THE DEATH DECISION

The Death Decision

Edited by Leonard J. Nelson

SERVANT BOOKS
Ann Arbor, Michigan

Copyright © 1984 by Oral Roberts University

Cover and book design by John B. Leidy

Available from Servant Publications, Box 8617, Ann Arbor,
   Michigan 48107

ISBN 0-89283-144-8

1 2 3 4 5 6 7 8 9 87 86 85 84

Printed in the United States of America

Contents

Preface

THESE ESSAYS EMANATED from papers presented at the Fourth Annual Christianity and Law Seminar presented November 11-13, 1982, at the City of Faith Continuing Education Center in Tulsa, Oklahoma. The seminar was sponsored by the O.W. Coburn School of Law of Oral Roberts University.

The O.W. Coburn School of Law, founded in 1979, was established through the generosity of O.W. Coburn, founder of Coburn Optical Industries. The law school is committed to merging Christianity with law in a new and unique manner. As a part of that commitment, the Annual Christianity and Law Seminar was established in 1980 to bring together mature scholars from various disciplines to reflect on specific problems resulting from the interaction of law and religion.

Previous seminars have dealt with the following topics: Christianity, Law, and Mediation: Roots and Relationships; A Christian Perspective on Ethics in Law; and Church, Family, State, and Education. The proceedings of the 1980-82 seminars have been published in the *Journal of Christian Jurisprudence.*

Participants in previous seminars have included Russell Kirk, one of America's leading thinkers; Lynn Buzzard, Executive Director of the Christian Legal Society; Errol Rohr, Presbyterian university pastor at Ohio State University; Thomas Morgan, Dean of the Emory University School of Law; William Ball, one of the leading experts in Church-State litigation; and Raymond O'Brien, a Catholic priest and assistant dean at Catholic University School of Law.

The primary impetus behind the Bioethics and Law Seminar was the 1982 opening of the City of Faith, a medical complex including a hospital, clinic, and research center dedicated to the merging of prayer and medicine. Because of the presence of the

City of Faith, and the practical need to confront various bioethical dilemmas, it was deemed expedient to devote the Annual Christianity and Law Seminar to that theme. As with other papers in this series, the essays in this volume represent the views of the various authors and not necessarily the views of the O.W. Coburn School of Law or Oral Roberts University.

We trust that you will also be stimulated and challenged as you read these essays.

Charles A. Kothe, Dean
O.W. Coburn School of Law

Contributors

Harold O.J. Brown is professor of systematic theology at Trinity Evangelical Divinity School. He has served as associate editor of both *Christianity Today* and *Human Life Review*. His books include *The Protest of a Troubled Protestant* and *Christianity and the Class Struggle*.

John Eidsmoe is visiting associate professor at O.W. Coburn School of Law, Oral Roberts University. He is author of *The Christian Legal Advisor*. He holds a Master of Divinity from Lutheran Brethren Seminary and a Master of Arts in biblical studies from Dallas Theological Seminary.

Leonard J. Nelson III, the editor of this book, was associate professor at O.W. Coburn School of Law, Oral Roberts University. In 1983-84 he was a Graduate Fellow at Yale Law School.

John T. Noonan is professor of law at the University of California, Berkeley. His books include *Contraception* and *A Private Choice*.

Walter Probert is professor at the University of Florida Law School and College of Medicine. His books include *Law, Language, and Communication*.

Charles E. Rice is professor at the University of Notre Dame Law School. His books include *Authority and Rebellion* and *Beyond Abortion*.

Peter J. Riga is professor of law at South Texas College of Law, Houston, Texas. His books include *The Death of the American Republic* and *The Right to Live or the Right to Die*.

George Huntston Williams is Hollis Professor of Divinity, Emeritus, at Harvard University. A former president of Americans United for Life, his books include *The Radical Reformation* and *Philosophy of John Paul II*.

Editor's Introduction

THE ESSAYS IN THIS VOLUME explore some of the moral and legal dilemmas arising from technological advances in biomedics and the disappearance of a Judeo-Christian consensus upon which to base our laws. The specific topics dealt with here come from both ends of the life spectrum: abortion, amniocentesis, infanticide, and euthanasia.

The contributors to this volume are all committed Christians, approaching their topics from various confessional perspectives: Messrs. Brown, Probert, Williams, and Eidsmoe are members of various Protestant churches; Messrs. Rice, Noonan, Riga, and Nelson are Roman Catholics.

Furthermore, the contributors also approach their topics from various professional perspectives: Messrs. Nelson, Rice, and Probert are law professors without formal theological training; Professor Williams is a renowned church historian, a fourth-generation ordained minister, and holder of the oldest and most prestigious Protestant theological chair, the Hollis Divinity Professorship; Professor Brown is a theologian; Professor Noonan is a law professor, canon law expert, and church historian; Professor Riga is a law professor who has also taught theology and holds advanced theological degrees, and Professor Eidsmoe is a law professor, scripture scholar, and ordained minister in the Lutheran Brethren Church.

The first three essays examine various perspectives on abortion. In the opening essay John Noonan focuses on the early church's position with respect to contraception and abortion and applies these norms to the problems of in vitro fertilization. John Eidsmoe then analyzes the biblical position on abortion from a fundamentalist perspective. Leonard

Nelson's essay examines the involvement of various modern churches in the controversy surrounding the legalization of abortion.

The next two essays explore the dilemmas arising from technological advances in biomedics as applied to the beginning of human life. In his essay on amniocentesis, Charles Rice explores the legal and moral dilemmas which have resulted from the ability of physicians to identify but not cure fetal anomalies. Peter Riga's essay surveys the legal and moral dilemmas resulting from the improved viability of defective neonates.

The third series of essays focuses on the moral and legal dilemmas at the other end of the life spectrum: those arising from technological advances in the prolongation of life. These dilemmas are perhaps some of the most difficult to resolve from a Christian perspective because of the potential contradiction between the traditional Christian reverence for human life and the Christian hope of life to come after death. Professor Harold Brown develops these themes in an essay which gives the reader a valuable framework for analyzing the morality, from a Christian perspective, of various types of euthanasia. Walter Probert's essay analyzes several judicial decisions illustrating the response of the legal system to the increasing ability of the medical profession to prolong life.

The concluding essay by George Huntston Williams is both scholarly and practical. It begins with a discussion of the origins of the term "bioethics," then provides an analytical framework for resolving various bioethical dilemmas, and concludes with a practical suggestion: the establishment of decisional bodies staffed by specially trained lawyers, physicians, and ethicists, who would resolve bioethical problems in specific cases by applying certain prescribed middle axioms derived from natural law precepts. The overriding theme of Professor Williams is the need for caution on the frontiers of biomedical research.

We hope these essays will assist the reader in resolving the difficult and sensitive bioethical issues that will continue to

arise as a result of the New Biology, which holds both promise
and peril for humanity.

> Leonard J. Nelson, III
> New Haven, Connecticut
> October, 1983

ONE

Christian Tradition and the Control of Human Reproduction

John T. Noonan, Jr.

N O SOCIETY HAS EVER BEEN indifferent to its continuance by reproduction or understood the methods and measures of reproduction to be a matter of private choice. The Christian religion, so closely concerned with human destiny on earth, has contributed to the social understanding of reproduction in each society in which Christianity has had a part; and to a substantial degree it formed the American legal framework of reproduction. Today, when this framework has been impaired by a series of decisions of the United States Supreme Court and when Christian teaching on sexual subjects is rejected by one part of American society, it is useful to look at the history of two Christian moral doctrines bearing on reproduction and to relate them to one set of social problems that now confront us in the New Biology. I propose accordingly to provide brief accounts of the Christian teaching on contraception and on abortion and then to relate both doctrines to the problems presented by in vitro fertilization.

Speaking of doctrine historically, I shall make three preliminary points. First, rules are responses—they are responses

1

to problems, they are answers to questions. To understand the rule is to understand the problems it addressed, the questions it answered. A rule, like any text, cannot be grasped apart from context. A rule does not exist *in vacuo,* in the air, apart from its surroundings. This is to say, in other words, that rules are made by persons with purposes. Purpose makes rules intelligible. Second, fidelity to a rule is fidelity to purpose, not to the mechanical letter of the rule. Questions change. To give the same answers to new questions is not fidelity but stupidity. Third, when new problems arise, they can be answered by analogies drawn from the old rule. An effort is necessary to isolate the values predominant in the old rule, to understand the purposes of its promulgators, and to preserve these values, these purposes, in a new response to a new question.

Let me now turn to the history of Christian teaching on contraception. The teaching condemning contraceptive practices is ancient, at least as old as the fourth century, arguably earlier.[1] The condemnation is a reaction or response to four evils. I shall enumerate these in order of significance, from the least important to the most.

The first of these evils was the association in the ancient Mediterranean world between contraception and illicit sexual intercourse. The Jews, Greeks, and Romans possessed contraceptive drugs and techniques. They hoped they worked. They used them in fornication, prostitution, or adultery to prevent unwanted consequences of their sexual activity. Christians, valuing sexual conduct only in the context of marriage, reacted negatively to means which accompanied and facilitated extramarital intercourse.[2]

The second evil was the position of women in a patriarchal society. In this Mediterranean world of slavery, slave concubinage, prostitution, and homosexual practice, it was easy to regard women as objects designed for male pleasure. Paradoxical as it may appear to modern educated women, means which kept women childless deprived them of their chief claim to status, that of being mothers. Motherhood was the key to the dignity of women. Christians, coming with a radical belief in the sexual equality of the sexes, as affirmed by St. Paul in First Corinthians, chapter 7, rejected means which appeared to deprive women of a unique function and so of their dignity and status.[3]

Third, and of ever greater importance, was the association of contraception with abortion. Abortion was in use on a large scale. There was no legal barrier to abortion with the consent of the father. The Christians, from the first century on, rejected abortion as an unqualified evil. Pressing their judgment against the law and medical practice of their day, they often phrased their condemnation of abortion so that it included contraception as well. This result occurred for both technical and theological reasons. Technically, it was difficult for even the most learned gynecologists to distinguish between abortifacients and contraceptives: there was simply not enough information available as to how antifertility drugs worked. Theologically, it was believed that ensoulment did not occur before the fortieth day in a male embryo (before the eightieth in a female). Consequently there was a period where the status of the being who was affected by the use of antifertility measures was less than human; yet there was Christian objection to its destruction. The defense of life easily extended to protect this period by banning contraceptive means.[4]

The final and most important of the evils to which the teaching on contraceptive practice was a response was the belief that procreation itself was evil or at any rate purposeless. This was in the first instance the belief among certain Christians of the first century who rejected both the Jewish and the Greek reasons for reproduction. The Jewish reason for reproduction was to perpetuate the race until the Messiah came. But these Christians thought the Messiah had come. Why continue the species? The Greek reason for reproduction was to overcome death, to attain immortality in one's children. But these Christians thought we are assured of immortality by the Resurrection. What need to seek a specious, surrogate immortality when we personally will never die? With both Greek and Jewish reasons rejected, two different attitudes to sexuality—

even then designated as those of the left and of the right—were manifested. On the right were those who said Christ's celibacy is example for us all. Every disciple must follow the Lord in abstaining absolutely from sexual intercourse. We are called to follow him in renouncing marriage. "Woe to whose who are with child in those days," the Lord had said in Luke 21:23; Matthew 24:19. These words, these Christians said, were, like other "Woe unto you," a curse—a curse on childbearing in "those days," that is, the days when the Messiah had come, the days now, in fact, at hand. On the left were Christians who asserted that Christ had abolished all the Mosaic commandments. When the Lord said, "The sabbath is made for man, not man for the sabbath" (Mk 2:27), he showed how even the sabbatarian precept should be subordinated to human needs; and if the worship of God could be subordinated in this way, so could lesser commandments regarding sex. The Christians of the left claimed liberty in general, and what they sometimes asserted in particular was sexual liberty. One of the several sects on the left was known as "Lords of the Sabbath," distinguished by their sexual freedom; and promiscuity was a characteristic running through various groups of the left.[5]

In the center, rejecting left and right, was the main body of Christians, who accepted marriage as good and lawful and the only proper place for sexual activity. In part, they found their answer to the left and right in Jewish tradition and in the Christian link to the Old Testament with its emphasis on procreation. In part they answered the basic question of the purpose of procreation by an appeal to nature—to nature as understood by Stoic thought. As the eye is to see, the Stoics taught, so the generative organs are to generate. The satisfaction of natural purpose is the justification and rationale for marriage and the proper measure of sexual conduct. The Stoic answer was adopted for the Christians by Clement of Alexandria, and this answer, giving a purpose to sexual activity yet limiting it to procreative acts, became the dominant answer among Christian moralists of the patristic period. It perfectly excluded contraception.[6]

The trauma of the early division between Left and Right over the purpose of sexual activity was reinforced by the experience of fourth-century Christianity. At this time, just as Christianity emerged from underground and became the religion of the Roman Empire, it was challenged by a new, underground, fast-spreading religion, organized with a hierarchy and presenting a sacred text—Manicheanism. It was a central story of the Manichees that there was once a King of Light in a kingdom of light and a King of Darkness in a kingdom of darkness. The King of Darkness was drawn to the light and, accompanied by his sons, invaded the kingdom of light; and the King of Light did battle with the King of Darkness, and the King of Light was defeated. The princes of darkness then devoured the princes of light and, returning to their own kingdom, copulated with the princesses of darkness; and from the union of devils there issued man. So man is the child of devils, but contains within himself particles of light representing the original sons of the King of Light. All of the rest of creation is then a rescue of the light particles. The King of Light has returned to his kingdom. He, the Father of Lights, awaits the return of the light particles. The one great sin is to imitate man's devilish ancestors and to procreate, because procreation perpetuates the imprisonment of the light.[7]

This myth in its essential sense of alienation from the world, in its essential rejection by an enlighted elite of God's creation, is not so different from certain currents of elitist, alienated thought recognizable in our own culture. In its own day it was sufficiently subtle and powerful to attract the minds of many thousands of believers and the most influential Christian writer on sexual morals, Augustine of Hippo, who was for eleven years a Manichee. The greatest effect of Augustine's long immersion in this thought was the depth and passion of his rejection of it after his conversion. The first book Augustine wrote after his conversion was *The Morals of the Manichees and the Morals of the Catholic Church,* and the great difference between Manichean morality and Catholic morality was found by Augustine to rest on their views of procreation. The Manichees maintained, Augustine reported, that prostitution was better than marriage because a prostitute was certain to take steps to prevent conception. The Catholics, on the other hand, believed that the only purpose justifying the seeking of marital intercourse was procreation. Restated with the brilliance and personal passion of Augustine, the rule of procreative purpose became the dominant approach in Christian moral thought for the next thirteen hundred years.[8]

I have said enough, perhaps, to indicate how specific evils generated specific responses and rejections. Positively interpreted, these responses may be summarized in four propositions:

(1) Procreation is good.
(2) Innocent life is not to be attacked.
(3) The personal dignity of each spouse is to be respected.
(4) Sexual love expressed in marriage is holy.

These four propositions converged. The rule rejecting contraception was a crystallization, a point of convergence, for the values embodied in these judgments.

One caveat must be added to avoid misunderstanding. Despite the Christian defense of procreation as cooperation with God's creation, the Christian position was never "the more, the merrier," never that an increase in the quantity of human beings was itself an objective. Rather, from the time of Clement of Alexandria onwards, procreation for Christians was always linked to education—that is, to the upbringing of children by their parents as religious and moral human beings. In the classic medieval formula, the good or value of children consisted in their procreation *and* education. Consequently, the mere multiplication of offspring—say by multiple acts of fornication—was never ranked as a good, but, rather, as an evil. Not the mere production of human beings but the production of human beings by loving parents who could bring them up was the Christian norm. Contraception was a rule protecting basic values; it was not a philoprogenitive prescription.[9]

The rule against contraception was neither criticized nor

challenged by Christians before the twentieth century. It was accepted without qualification by Greek Orthodox, Roman Catholics, and Protestants, and indeed it was supported by doctors, scientists, and legislators as well. Only in 1930 did change begin within the Christian community. The Anglican Church led the way in 1930. By 1960 most of the major Protestant churches had accepted the lawfulness of contraception within marriage. For these churches—with no repudiation of the basic values of procreation, the sanctity of innocent life, the personal dignity of the spouses, and the holiness of conjugal sexuality—the old absolute prohibition did not need to be maintained.[10]

Within the Catholic Church, too, in the 1960s there was a restudying of the old ban. The result was two documents, the pastoral constitution *Gaudium et spes* of the Second Vatican Council, and the encyclical *Humanae Vitae* issued by Paul VI in 1968. The Council taught that one good and lawful purpose of conjugal intercourse, apart from procreation, was the expression of conjugal love—a definite rejection of the old Alexandrian-Augustinian position on the necessity of procreative purposes. But the Pope taught that "every act whatsoever" by which procreation is intentionally excluded is immoral.[11]

To some readers of the Pope his encyclical was a repetition of the absolute prohibition of contraception for Catholics. Other commentators have read the encyclical differently. The Pope gave a new reason for the prohibition—that the nexus between the expression of conjugal love and procreative power had been established by God and so should not be tampered with by man.[12] This reason gave a purpose for the prohibition which at the same time limited it. The prohibition held for every period in which, by the laws of nature, fertility could be expected. In every such period there was a divinely established connection between an act of marital intercourse expressing love and procreation. But the prohibition did not hold for every period which was naturally infertile. In every such period there was a natural separation of fertility from the expression of conjugal love.[13]

Building on that separation, Paul VI himself made clear that he did not speak literally and absolutely when he said "every act whatsoever," because he himself raised no objection to acts of human intelligence by which periods of natural infecundity would be established.[14] And going beyond this official acceptance of the rhythm method of contraception, it has been plausibly argued that any use of other contraceptive means to secure the natural periods of infertility falls within what is permitted by the encyclical. The ban on contraception is by this reasoning limited to the four days per cycle in which fertility is naturally present.[15]

Christian teaching then has very largely developed from the position of the first centuries; it has always sought to preserve the same basic values. It does not exclude certain human calculations designed to assure sterility. Let me now turn to abortion.

Abortion, as I have indicated, was rejected from the first century on. Indeed its rejection is arguably—even probably—made in scripture itself. The key term is *pharmakeia,* often rendered in English as "magic" or "sorcery" but meaning in the texts in which it is used "the practice of abortion by drugs." In Galatians 5:20, along with "lecheries" and "wraths" the rejected works of the flesh include *pharmakeia.* In Apocalypse 9:21 those who use *pharmakeia* are among the unrepentant sinners. In Apocalypse 21:8 the *pharmakoi* are condemned with the murderers and the fornicators. In Apocalypse 22:18, the dogs (that is, the sodomites), the fornicators, and the murderers are outside the heavenly city, and with them are the *pharmakoi,* those who practice abortion by drug.[16]

The same theme appears in the *Didache* or *Teaching of the Twelve Apostles,* a first-century work. Among the commandments given here are "You shall not kill. You shall not commit adultery. You shall not corrupt boys. You shall not fornicate. You shall not steal. You shall not make magic. You shall not practice *pharmakeia.*" And in the Way of Death set out by this book are the sinners who practice *pharmakeia* and those who are "killers of the child, who abort the mold of God." The offense of abortion is seen as an offense against God because it attacks what he has created; and it is seen as an offense against the love of neighbor because it is a type of killing.[17]

The prohibition of abortion is a hallmark of Christians in the early centuries. It is an absolute prohibition. Only in the Middle Ages was it relaxed by consideration of therapeutic abortion to save the life of the mother. First the minority opinion of the Dominican, Giovanni of Naples, this view gained currency until by the time of Alfonso de' Ligouri in the eighteenth century it was accepted as a probable view at least prior to the time of ensoulment of the embryo. The law also accepted this position, a Christian country like England having made abortion of an ensouled fetus criminal since the thirteenth century but permitting abortion to save the life of the mother.[18]

Two major developments in the teaching occurred in the nineteenth century. The first was the acceptance of a New Biology, which rejected the old view of Aristotle that there were stages of fetal development before the human species was reached at the fortieth or eightieth day. The New Biology—actually as old as the seventeenth century, but very gradually accepted by law, medicine, and theology—saw human beings coming into existence at conception. The law was accordingly changed to ban abortion from conception, and theological teaching was amended to make clear that any abortion, at whatever stage of pregnancy, was the taking of human life.[19] The other development was pastoral and conservative. In the face of an increasing number of therapeutic abortions, and the danger of the therapeutic rationale being abused, the Catholic Church imposed on Catholics a ban of therapeutic abortions. Nonetheless, even the Catholic ban was not quite absolute: it was admitted that, in the case of ectopic pregnancy, abortion to save the mother's life was permissible.[20]

As matters stood in the mid 1960s, all major Christian churches condemned abortion, and all American states had in effect well-established laws prohibiting all but therapeutic abortions. Thanks to major efforts by the American Civil Liberties Union and Planned Parenthood of America, the laws began to change, and in 1973 all of the laws were annulled by decision of the Supreme Court.[21] The Christian churches have now divided on the legal issue, some holding that civil law need not or should not enforce the religious objection to killing the unborn. No major Christian theologian, to my knowledge, has held that a Christian can take the life of the unborn except where the life of the mother is at stake. As the exception exists, the value of innocent unborn life is not quite absolute. But it is as close to being an absolute as an earthly value can be. Abortion attacks this value. In the words of Karl Barth abortion is "the great modern sin."[22]

What is at stake in the Christian churches' rejection of abortion has perhaps been no better expressed than by a man who, although reared in a Christian culture, was not himself a believer, André Gide. I quote from his *Last Journals*:

When morning came, "get rid of that," I said naively to the gardener's wife when she finally came to see how everything was. Could I have supposed that those formless fragments, to which I, turning away in disgust was pointing, could I have supposed that in the eyes of the Church they already represented the sacred human being they were being readied to clothe? O mystery of incarnation! Imagine then my stupor when some hours later I saw "it" again. That thing which for me already had no name in any language, now cleaned, adorned, beribboned, laid in a little cradle, awaiting the ritual entombment. Fortunately no one had been aware of the sacrilege I had been about to commit; I had already committed it in thought when I had said get rid of "that." Yes, very happily that ill-considered order had been heard by no one. And, I remained a long time musing before "it." Before that little face and the crushed forehead on which they they had carefully hidden the wound. Before this innocent flesh which I, if I had been alone, yielding to my first impulse, would have consigned to the manure heap along with the afterbirth and which religious attentions had just saved from the void. I told no one then of what I felt. Of what I tell here. Was I to think that for a few moments a soul had inhabited this body? It has its tomb in Couvreville in that cemetery to which I wish not to return. Half a century has passed. I cannot say that I recall in detail that little face. No. What I remember exactly is my surprise, my sudden emotion, when confronted by its extraordinary beauty.[23]

Reverence for human life, for one's neighbor, for God's image in God's creation—Gide has captured these values in his unforgettable words; and they are at the heart of the Christian position.

Now I turn to my third task, to ask what we can learn from the Christian tradition when we confront IVF (In Vitro Fertilization) or as it is sometimes called EHF (External Human Fertilization) or VIP (Vital Initiation of Pregnancy). First let us look at the facts.

In VIP, as I shall call it, a maturing ovum is located by laparoscopy and is by gentle suction removed from the ovary. The egg is put in a laboratory dish and introduced to sperm. Fertilization takes place. After two or three days of observation the fertilized ovum is inserted into the maternal uterus. The entire operation has avoided blockage of the egg in the oviducts and has achieved insemination. Since 1978, well over one hundred of such operations have been undertaken.[24]

If the egg is intentionally destroyed at any point after being fertilized, abortion occurs, and the Christian moral judgment of condemnation is evidently required—the unusual means used do not deprive these human beings of their sacred character or subject them to the will of those who helped to produce them. In the first years of VIP, when there was concern about the kind of human VIP would produce, abortion was seen as a technique ready to be used if the fertilized egg showed signs of being defective. But clearly the operation described is in itself neither contraception nor abortion. It would be a mistake to try to pin such labels on it. It may be that we can learn to think about it from our tradition on contraception and abortion.

Three issues are posed by the operation. Let me enumerate them.

(1) the risk of harm to the child conceived in this way—is it unacceptable?

(2) the interference with the natural processes of ovulation—is it in derogation of the divine plan?

(3) the production of the fertilizing sperm—is it obtained immorally by an act that should be characterized as against nature?

The first question, I suggest, may be answered in Christian terms by our general valuation of human life as better than nonbeing. Even though a child should be born with defects or should live only a short time, he or she is better off alive than nonexistent. To bring anyone into the world is to prepare someone for death. Yet our mothers are not our murderers. I do not see a Christian objection to the conception itself as long as the purpose is to produce a new human life to be brought up as a human being.

The second question can be answered in terms of the traditional Christian willingness to accept therapeutic correction of natural defects. The removal and replacement of the egg are done to correct an unnatural blockage of the fallopian tubes. In these actions, considered by themselves, natural processes are not frustrated, but assisted.

The third question on the morality of artificial insemination presents the most difficulty. The position taken by Pope Pius XII is that artificial measures may be used to assist insemination only if they are used to complete an act of natural intercourse; Pius XII treated as illegitimate the production of sperm apart from such an act, even though the sperm were to be used subsequently for fertilization.[25] Clearly we are in an area where disagreement may be expected. The Pope proceeded by judging the sperm-producing action as a moral unit in itself without regard to its purpose of furthering fertilization. Opinions can and do differ as to whether this judgment of the isolated physical act is correct. Even by Pius XII's stringent standard, there can be no objection to sperm collection at the time of a natural act of intercourse and the use of this sperm for fertilization. In short, the use of techniques to inseminate is not in itself objectionable, even though dispute continues as to what techniques are acceptable.

Let us consider a more complex and more controversial case. Suppose that instead of one ovum being extracted at a time of a laparoscopy, the follicles are hormonally stimulated and multiple ova are produced and sucked out. This is in fact what is now done at Norfolk.[26] Two problems are presented. One is the artificial stimulation of ovulation to produce several eggs. The other is what happens to the surplus.

The first problem is not serious. The stimulation of ovulation is a reinforcement of natural processes, akin to the natural superabundance that produces twins. The second problem is severe if the surplus eggs are fertilized. If they remain unfertilized and stored, no special problem exists. But present-day technology favors fertilization before storage, and this is in fact done, resulting in the conception of new human beings. At one VIP facility these extra new human beings are then put in cold storage, to be used later if needed.[27] Is this treatment of actual human life defensible? If there is no other alternative way of continuing the existence of these beings, storage cannot be wrong—at least their lives are saved. The morality of producing a surplus, however, can be called into question since Christian tradition has never taught "the more the better," but has always insisted that procreation be linked to the upbringing of those procreated. A number of the human beings created in this way have little chance of further upbringing. Their procreation would appear to be as wrong by Christian standards as the mindless procreation of offspring by fornication.

Is the case altered if, instead of being stored, the fertilized ova, these actual human beings, are all inserted in the mother's womb? This is the present policy at Norfolk.[28] The result is occasional twinning, but more often the development of only one conceptus while the others die. The reason for adopting this approach is that it apparently increases the probability of successful implantation. It is a kind of imitation of the surplus energy of nature which sometimes achieves its end by producing more fertilized eggs than will survive. As the purpose of the act when all the fertilized eggs are put in the womb is to give the possibility of development to as many as can naturally survive, I do not see that the artificial process is more disrespectful to human life than the natural process is; and the Norfolk protocol is, in that respect, acceptable to Christian judgment.

Further possibilities for the technology exist, as yet, so far as reported literature goes, untried. Here are three. One: an egg after fertilization is inserted in the womb of a woman not the donor of the egg; at birth the surrogate mother returns the baby to the genetic mother. Two: sperm from an anonymous donor is used to fertilize an egg from an anonymous donor; the fertilized egg is incubated in a surrogate mother's womb. Three: the same anonymous production of human life as in two, followed by biological experimentation on the human being produced in order to understand early embryonic development and to prevent disease and defects detectable at the early stages of life. Are any of these methods acceptable to Christians?

The first possibility separates gestation from motherhood, but ultimately restores the baby to the genetic mother. It is analogous to the old custom of using women other than the mother to give milk to a new baby. If medically necessary, it seems to be unobjectionable. The acceptance of this possibility, however, can be the wedge opening the way to a complete severance between the genetic progenitors and the actual deliverer of the child.

This possibility, the second case, is best considered on its merits. It divorces procreation entirely from marriage. Anonymous donors become breeders. This is the ultimate violation of what Paul VI has defended as the divine plan yoking procreative power to the expression of conjugal love. Its acceptance brings us to the worlds of Huxley and Orwell in which the final trick is played on the champions of procreation as a private choice: the state, necessarily and inevitably, takes charge of all breeding. The process is profoundly contrary to values of human dignity and marital love cherished by Christians.

The third possibility, the breeding of human beings for

experimentation, appeals sentimentally to the medical good that may be done while it wickedly exploits human beings as objects. It proposes acts of ultimate irreverence to the human lives the Christian church has always held sacred. To this possibility of degrading human life the answer of Christians must always be an unyielding no; and to avoid reaching that condition of society where such breeding of human beings as objects becomes routine, the Christian insistence that pro-creation is indissolubly linked to conjugal love is the first and most significant safeguard.

TWO

A Biblical View of Abortion

John A. Eidsmoe

A WELL-KNOWN COMEDIAN once said he had heard jokes about every political subject one could imagine, from capital punishment to war and peace, but never a joke about abortion. The reason, he suggested, is that abortion arouses such strong emotions in people of all viewpoints, that it simply isn't funny to anyone. Indeed, there is probably no political or moral issue that grips people like abortion does. It is anomalous, however, that in a society where a majority of the American people claim to honor the Bible as the Word of God, few spokesmen on either side focus on biblical teaching concerning abortion. For those who do not accept the Bible as authoritative, that is understandable. But those who do accept the authority of scripture should certainly ask themselves, does the Bible give us any guidance concerning the morality of abortion?

Although there is no scriptural passage that specifically says, "Thou shalt not have an abortion," there are passages of scripture touching upon abortion or having clear implications concerning abortion. If these passages are synthesized, they establish that abortion is contrary to the Word of God.

The basic moral principle involved is the commandment of Exodus 20:13: "Thou shalt not kill." The Hebrew word used for kill in Exodus 20:13 is *ratsach,* which usually means an intentional and unjustified killing of a human being. Not all killing is murder, however, and for other types of killings, e.g., accidental deaths, killing in war, killing in self-defense, or the execution of criminals, different Hebrew words are used, such as *katal* and *harag*.

The initial question posed is whether the biblical injunction "thou shalt not kill" applies to abortion. The commandment prohibits the intentional and unjustified killing of a human being and clearly abortion often is intentional. The difficult questions, however, are (1) Does abortion involve the killing of a human being and (2) if so, when if ever is it justifiable?

I. Is the Unborn Child a Human Being?

Various passages of scripture implicitly touch upon the question of when human life begins.[1] For example, the Hebrew and Greek used in ancient manuscripts typically make no distinction between the unborn child and children who are already born.

Various Hebrew and Greek words which are used in the Bible for the unborn child are:

(1) *Brephos*—*Brephos* is a Greek word used for baby. The term is used for "babe" in Luke 1:44, where Elizabeth says of her unborn child, John the Baptist, "the *babe* [*brephos*] in my womb leaped for joy." In the next chapter, the angel says to the shepherds, "ye shall find the *babe* [*brephos*] wrapped in swaddling clothes, lying in a manger" (Lk 2:12).

In First Timothy 3:15, Paul states, "From a *child* [*brephos*] thou hast known the holy scriptures. . . ."

Thus, the authors of scripture make no distinction in the use of the word *brephos*: it is used for an unborn child in Luke 1, for a child already born in Luke 2, and for a young child in 1 Timothy.

(2) *Huios*—*Huios* is a Greek word commonly used for son. In Luke 1:36, the angel tells Mary, "Thy cousin, Elizabeth, hath also conceived a *son* [*huios*]." Five verses earlier in Luke 1:31, the angel told Mary, "thou shalt conceive in thy womb, and bring forth a son [*huios*]." And two chapters later, God the Father says to the Lord Jesus Christ, "Thou art my beloved *Son*

[*huios*]" (Lk 3:22). And at this time, Jesus was a young adult. Again, the New Testament makes no distinction between an unborn child and a child already born in the use of the word *huios*.

(3) *Ben—Ben* is a Hebrew word commonly translated as son or child. It appears hundreds of times in scripture, normally for a child already born, but not always. In Genesis 25:21-24, we read of Jacob and Esau in the womb of their mother, Rebekah: "And the *children* [*ben*] struggled within her. . . ." It is used to refer to Ishmael when he was 13 years old (Gn 17:25) and for Noah's adult sons (Gn 9:19).

(4) *Gehver—Gehver* is used approximately 65 times in scripture, usually for a man or men. However, Job 3:3 states: "Let the day perish wherein I was born, and the night in which it was said, there is a *manchild* [*gehver*] conceived."

(5) *Gohlahl—Gohlahl* is used on twenty occasions in scripture, and in most instances it refers to a child already born: e.g., Lamentations 4:4 states: "The young children [*gohlahl*] ask bread." In contrast, Job 3:16 refers to "*infants* [*gohlahl*] which never saw light." Clearly, in that context, *gohlahl* means unborn children.

This linguistic analysis is significant insofar as it shows the same terminology being used for the unborn child and for the child already in being. It indicates that the authors of scripture regard the unborn child as a human being.

Biblical authors also identify themselves with the unborn child. Psalm 139:13-16: "Thou hast covered *me* in my mother's womb." It does not say thou hast covered the fetus that became me, or thou hast covered my embryo. Rather, the author identifies himself with the unborn child in the womb. Moreover, Isaiah 49:1 states: "The Lord hath called *me* from the womb," and Jeremiah 1:5 states: "before *thou* camest forth out of the womb, I sanctified *thee* and I ordained *thee* a prophet unto the nations." Thus the author identifies the prophets as children in the womb.

In some cases the author of scripture attributes sin to the unborn child. For example in Psalm 51:5 states: "Behold, I was

shapen in iniquity; and in sin did my mother conceive me."
This does not necessarily mean that the act of conception is
sinful. It could also indicate that the child has a sin nature from
the time of conception. This attribution of sin to the unborn
child indicates that the unborn child is a person, not a mass of
tissue.[2]

Another passage often used to support a scriptural view of the
unborn child as human being is Luke 1:44, which states, "the
babe in my womb leaped for joy," indicating that Elizabeth's
child, John the Baptist, leaped for joy in the womb when in the
presence of Mary who was carrying Jesus in her womb. This is
an expression of emotion and recognition of personhood.

Finally, Genesis 25:22 states, concerning Esau and Jacob
within the womb of Rebecca, "And the children struggled
together within her." This, again, is a sign of personhood.

The Bible also affords a basis for giving legal protection to the
unborn child. Exodus 21:22-25 is probably the passage of
scripture which speaks most directly to the question of
abortion. However, many shy away from the use of this passage
because of its apparent ambiguity. It reads:

> If men strive, and hurt a woman with child, so that her fruit
> depart from her, and yet no mischief follow: he shall be surely
> punished, according as the woman's husband will lay upon
> him; and he shall pay as the judges determine. And if any
> mischief follow, then thou shall give life for life, eye for eye,
> tooth for tooth, hand for hand, foot for foot, burning for
> burning, wound for wound, stripe for stripe."[3]

The key phrase is in verse 22: "her fruit depart from her."
Some translations, including the New American Standard,
render fruit as "miscarriage." However, the Hebrew is *yehled*
which is found many times in the Old Testament. In every other
place, it refers to a human being—a child, children, a boy, or a
young man. In no other passage is it used for anything less than
a human being.

The Hebrew word for depart is "yatsah." In most other

passages where this verb appears in connection with childbirth, it refers to a live birth.[4] If Moses had wanted to speak about a miscarriage, there are at least two distinctive Hebrew words available: (1) *shakol*—a word used for miscarriage in Exodus 23:26, and which also appears in Hosea 9:14; (2) *nephel,* a word used for miscarriage in Job 3:16, Psalm 58:8, and Ecclesiastes 6:3. Accordingly, Moses by using *yatsah* in Exodus 21:22 could be referring to a premature but live birth.

Ahsohn is the Hebrew word which is translated "mischief" in the King James Version. *Ahsohn* means mischief or harm and could refer to anything from death to a sore finger. *Ahsohn* could refer only to harm to the mother; or, since the passage could contemplate a live birth, *ahsohn* may refer to both the mother and to the child. When translated in this manner, the meaning of the passage is: If men are involved in a fight and hurt a pregnant woman so that she delivers her child prematurely, but there is no injury to the mother or child, the husband is to be compensated only for his time, expenses, inconvenience, etc., and perhaps pain and suffering as well. But if the mother or child is injured, as a result, or if either die as a result, the *lex talionis* or law of like punishment applies: eye for eye, tooth for tooth, life for life.

The medical evidence also affirms the humanity of the fetus. From the moment the sperm and egg come together to form a fertilized zygote, the child has a genetic makeup unique from that of his mother and father. If we could analyze that genetic makeup, we would know from conception the child's sex, hair color, bone structure, skin color, and many other traits.

Two weeks after conception, the child already has a blood supply and blood type. Its blood and the mother's blood come into contact through a membrane, but they do not mingle. By the end of the third week, the heart is beating and a body rhythm has been established that will last all the child's life. By the fourth week, the brain, arms, legs, kidneys, liver, and digestive tract have begun to take shape. At the end of the four weeks, the child is already 10,000 times larger than it was at conception. At the end of the second month, the child is still less than one thumb's length in size, but its hands, feet, head, organs, and brain are in place. There are even fingerprints!

During the third month of pregnancy, the palms of the child's hands become sensitive as do the soles of the feet. The child will grasp an object placed in its hand and make a fist, it swallows, parts its lips, furrows its brow, and moves to avoid light or pressure. The eyelids even squint. By the end of the third month, the child has fingernails, sucks its thumb, and recoils from pain. After the third month, the development of the child consists largely of growth and strengthening: all of the vital organs are already present.[5]

Dr. Paul E. Rockwell has related an amazing encounter:

> Years ago, while giving an anesthetic for a ruptured tubal pregnancy (at 2 months), I was handed what I believed to be the smallest human being ever seen. The embryo sac was intact and transparent. Within the sac was a tiny, 1/3-inch human male swimming extremely vigorously in the amniotic fluid, while attached to the wall by the umbilical cord. This tiny human was perfectly developed with long, tapering fingers, feet and toes. It was almost transparent, in regards to the skin, and the delicate arteries and veins were prominent to the ends of the fingers. The baby was extremely alive and did not look at all like the photos and drawings of "embryos" which I had seen. When the sac was opened, the tiny human immediately lost its life and took on the appearance of what is accepted as the appearance of an embryo at this stage, blunt extremities, etc.[6]

Not only does the unborn child have the physical character-istics of a human being; it also has distinctive personal characteristics: if the womb is touched with a sharp instrument, the child will draw away from the instrument and some will move more than others. Moreover, Verny and Kelly have established that if a child has been used to hearing its father's voice while in the womb, it may be able to pick it out in the first hour or two after birth and respond emotionally.[7]

Verny and Kelly also describe the experience of a young American mother who had lived in Toronto, Canada, during her pregnancy, and thereafter moved to Oklahoma City. One day, when her child was two years old, she was surprised to find the child sitting on the living room floor chanting, "Breathe in, breathe out, breathe in, breathe out"—the words of the Lamaze exercise for childbirth. The possibility that the child had picked up these words from a source such as television was dismissed as impossible, for those words are used only in the Canadian version, not the American version. There was only one possible exlanation: "the child had memorized the words while she was still in the womb."[8]

Verny and Kelly further quote Boris Brott, conductor of the Hamilton (Ontario) Philharmonic Symphony:

> . . . as a young man, I was mystified by this unusual ability I have—to play certain pieces sight unseen. I'd be conducting a score for the first time, and suddenly the cello line would jump out at me; I'd know the flow of the piece even before I turned the page of the score. One day, I mentioned this to my mother, who is a professional cellist. I thought she would be intrigued because it was always the cello line that was so distinct in my mind. She was; but when she heard what the pieces were, the mystery quickly solved itself. All the scores I knew sight unseen, were ones she had played while she was pregnant with me.[9]

II. Is Abortion Ever Justifiable?

Some argue that abortion is justified as an extension of equal rights for women, i.e., a woman's right to control her own body. However, the medical evidence clearly establishes the fetus is not part of the mother's body: rather it is a separate and distinct human being. If we assume the primary function of government is the protection of human life, then human life in the womb should be entitled to legal protection. Moreover, since the right to life is more basic and fundamental than the right of a woman to choose to terminate her pregnancy, the right to life should take precedence over the right to choose.

We have seen that the scripture, properly interpreted, establishes that individual human life begins at conception. There are four possible alternative viewpoints, none of which find support in scripture, as to when life begins: birth, viability, quickening, or implantation. The more difficult question, however, is at what point should legal protection for human life begin? It is clear biologically that a new life is present from the time of conception, and so the more profound question is at what point should we accord that life human dignity? In reality, the four oft-proposed alternatives to the point of conception as the beginning point of human life are alternatives as to when human life deserves legal protection.

The primary (and usually the only) Bible passage cited in support of abortion on demand is Genesis 2:7: "And the Lord God formed man of the dust of the ground, and breathed into his nostrils the breath of life; and man became a living soul." From this passage some fundamentalists argue that one is not completely human until he begins breathing, that is, at birth. However, an analysis of this verse does not support that position.

First, this is a unique, one-time event. The formation of Adam does not answer the question of whether human life begins in the womb, because in the Genesis account Adam was never in a womb. He was the first man, and he was formed out of the dust as an adult, mature human being. Even if we concede that in order to be fully human one must breathe air, the fact still remains that the unborn child uses oxygen: its oxygen is simple taken in a different manner before birth, i.e., through the placenta. In addition, there are certain medical procedures by which air is inserted into the womb, and occasionally the unborn child will take a gulp of air duing that procedure. In the final analysis, birth is simply a change of environment but it does not represent a significant change in the nature of the organism.

Viability refers to the ability of the child to sustain life outside the womb. Many argue that the unborn child becomes fully human at the point of viability and accordingly should not be afforded legal protection prior to that time. However, viability varies according to the neonatal care available: a generation ago, viability was generally thought to be about the sixth month after conception, but now because of improved neonatal care the premature infant is now often capable of surviving at the fifth month.

Thus, ultimately, viability is a subjective test: in many cases there is no way of knowing whether a child, given adequate medical treatment, could have survived outside the womb. And viability is not logically related to being fully human. For example, the child who is already born can survive for, at most, a few hours or a few days without someone to care for it. Accordingly, viability does not provide a basis for determining if a fetus should be regarded as deserving of legal protection.

Quickening is the point at which the mother first feels the unborn child move within her womb. Like viability, quickening is a subjective test because it depends upon the mother's feeling rather than actual movement: i.e., the fetus may move long before it is large enough or strong enough for its mother to feel its movement. In fact, there is cellular activity from the point of conception. Quickening also varies with individuals, and throughout pregnancy some children are simply more active than others. But this does not mean that some are deserving of legal protection sooner than others. Therefore, the test of quickening has no basis in logic or common sense.

Some have suggested that implantation is perhaps the only logical alternative to conception as the point when human life is deserving of legal protection. The implantation of the zygote/ embryo in the wall of the uterus occurs approximately seven days after fertilization. Prior to burrowing into the uterine wall, the zygote/embryo spends about three days in the fallopian tube and three days in the uterine cavity. About one-half of the cells that constitute the embryo at implantation specialize to form the placenta. Prior to implantation, an embryo could develop into twins. Thus, while acknowledging that human life develop into twins. Thus, while acknowledging that human life begins at conception, some Christians are reluctant to refer to a zygote prior to implantation as an individual human being. I believe, however, that an individual human life comes into existence at the time of conception and if twinning takes place subsequently then a second life comes into being.

It is often argued that abortion is justified in cases of pregnancy resulting from rape or incest. Fortunately, pregnancy as a result of rape happens far less frequently than is commonly supposed. A study reported in the *Illinois Medical Journal* found that there were no pregnancies resulting from rape in a 9-year period in Chicago.[10] Other reports show no pregnancies resulting from rape in over 30 years in Buffalo, New York,[11] none in over ten years in St. Paul, Minnesota,[12] and none in Philadelphia in a decade.[13] One reason is that more than one-third of rapists are either impotent or have premature or retarded ejaculation.[14] Pregnancies resulting from incest are similarly rare, and those pregnancies which result from incest and which are subsequently aborted are even more rare.[15]

Since they are very rare, pregnancies resulting from rape and incest should not be used to justify abortion on demand. And even if abortion is to be allowed for rape and incest, statutes should be narrowly drawn to limit abortion to those circumstances only, and such laws should have adequate safeguards to insure that the pregnancy has indeed resulted from genuine rape or incest and that this charge is not being used simply as an excuse to obtain an abortion solely for reasons of convenience.

Moreover, a law allowing abortion even for rape or incest overlooks the right of the child to choose life. It is certainly wrong to punish an innocent child for the sin of its father, and abortion does not undo the harm of rape or incest. Indeed, while having to bear an unwanted child can certainly be traumatic, abortion can be equally traumatic.

Abortion is also often justified as necessary to protect maternal mental health. However, there is little evidence that abortion enhances mental health. In fact, a study done at the University of British Columbia's Department of Psychiatry demonstrated that abortion often increases women's psychological stress.[16] Indeed, abortion may be more detrimental to a woman's mental health than bearing a child and putting him up for adoption. And even if it is conceded that abortion could improve the mental health of the mother, there is still a conflict of rights: the mother's right to mental health versus the child's right to life, and the right to life should be paramount.

It is sometimes argued that abortion will reduce child abuse in spite of a dearth of empirical evidence supporting this proposition. There is no evidence that unplanned or unwanted pregnancies result in a higher proportion of unwanted or abused children. On the contrary, as abortion statistics have skyrocketed over the past decade, instances of reported child abuse have similarly increased. Edward Lenoski, Professor of Pediatrics at the University of Southern California, who conducted an extensive study of over 1,300 battered children, discovered that 91% of these children were the result of planned pregnancies, 90% were legitimate, and 24% were named after their parents as compared to only 4% of a control group.[17]

This seems anomalous until we realize two important factors: (1) Parents often change their minds about wanting a child during or after pregnancy. An unplanned or unwanted pregnancy does not necessarily result in an unwanted or unloved child, or vice-versa. (2) Parents who abuse their children usually love their children just as much as other parents. The abuse stems not from lack of love, but from deep-seated psychological problems. Clearly, there is little reason to believe that abortion will solve the problem of unwanted or abused children.

Some contend abortion is justifiable in cases of severe fetal deformity. However, if you accept the premise that the fetus is a human being, there is no moral difference between killing before birth and killing after birth. Indeed, any argument for abortion based upon birth defects can be made with equal or greater force for infanticide.

Moreover, in most instances it is not possible to predict with any reasonable medical certainty the severity of fetal defects. Retardation, for example, may be extreme, slight, or nonexistent. Many persons with birth defects have lived happy and meaningful lives and have made valuable contributions to society. Finally, useful or not, wanted or not, normal or not, even the defective child has the right to life.

Abortions necessary to save the mother's life are the only abortions which may be justifiable. Fortunately, with modern medical techniques it is also an unusual situation. In cases where the mother's life is truly and imminently endangered by the pregnancy, there is a serious dilemma: the child's right to life versus the mother's right to life. Since the law normally does not require one person to give up life in order to preserve the life of another person, abortion to save the life of the mother should be permitted. An additional but extremely rare exception might be the case involving twins, where the abortion of one twin might be necessary to prevent two deaths.

This does not mean that all persons faced with this dilemma will opt for abortion. Some may believe that a deliberate act of killing is wrong under any circumstances, and such persons may choose to go through with the childbirth and leave the consequences to God. While this is a morally acceptable option, it should not be required by law.

THREE

The Churches and Abortion Law Reform

Leonard J. Nelson, III

THE MODERN CONTROVERSY over abortion in many ways parallels the historic controversy over slavery. It focuses on the meaning of personhood by requiring a determination of whether a particular category of persons are entitled to be treated as members of the human community. In the slavery controversy, the debate was over whether a Negro slave was a person. In the *Dred Scott v. Sandford*[1] decision, the U.S. Supreme Court determined that Negroes were not persons in the eyes of the law. This disastrous decision was eventually reversed by the Thirteenth and Fourteenth Amendments. Similarly, in *Roe v. Wade*[2] the U.S. Supreme Court determined that the unborn were not persons in the eyes of the law.

At the time of the slavery controversy, the churches were involved extensively on both sides of the controversy. The impetus of the abolitionist movement was largely religious: the Quakers were initially in the forefront of the movement, but they were soon joined by representatives of other major Protestant denominations. The defense of slavery was also undertaken by their coreligionists in the South, and both sides relied on scripture to justify their positions. The effect of the slavery controversy was to split many of the major Protestant denominations along regional lines.[3] The abortion controversy has also split the churches, not along regional lines or even denominational lines, but rather along philosophical lines.

Attitudes toward abortion are typically related to attitudes toward extramarital and premarital sex. Those who favor liberalized abortion also typically favor the repeal of laws prohibiting consensual sexual acts. Those favoring abortion on demand also usually favor widespread distribution of contraceptives to adolescents and programs of sex education. This viewpoint assumes that legal restrictions on abortion will be unenforceable and that legalized abortion is necessary to back up contraceptive failure.

The American Law Institute has asserted that objections to liberalized abortion laws are not primarily based on legal considerations but rather on religious beliefs which deem abortion sinful.[4] What the ALI failed to acknowledge, however, was that advocacy of liberalized abortion is also based on a religious view. In this regard, today's liberal Protestants, Reformed Jews, and dissenting Catholics are the spiritual heirs of the Manichees and the Albigensians. Their religiously based ethic regards the fetus as an evil which may be eradicated in order to serve a higher good. This higher good is the development of a society which allows the greatest possible personal freedom in sexual matters and enhances the quality of life by eliminating "unwanted" babies.

Until the 1960s, no mainline denomination took a position approving abortion on demand. Since the 1960s, however, several religious groups have become advocates for abortion. The Religious Coalition for Abortion Rights, which is coincidentally located in the United Methodist Church's building in Washington, D.C., has acted as a pro-abortion lobbyist for several of these religious groups. The RCAR has been characterized as "a joining together of religious organizations which have officially adopted the position that decisions concerning abortion should be made according to individual conscience."[5]

The RCAR cuts across religious lines to include Catholics,

Protestants, Jews, and secular humanists. Their common concern seems to be a commitment to federally funded abortion on demand. Its membership includes the Division of Social Ministries of the American Baptist Churches; the National Council of Jewish Women; the Union of American Hebrew Congregations; the Center for Social Action and the Board of Homeland Ministries of the United Church of Christ; the General Executive Board and the Commission on Women's Concerns of the Presbyterian Church in the United States; the Church and Society Unit, the Washington Office, and the Women's Program Unit of the United Presbyterian Church of the United States; the Unitarian-Universalist Association; the Board of Church and Society, and the Women's Division of the United Methodist Church; the Unitarian-Universalist Women's Federation; B'nai B'rith Women; Catholics for a Free Choice; the Washington Office of the Church of the Brethren; the National Federation of Temple Sisterhoods; the American Ethical Union; and the American Humanist Association.[6]

Another important multidenominational religious group among early proponents of an unrestricted right to abortion was the Clergy Consultation Service for Problem Pregnancies, which was organized in New York City in 1967 by a minister from the Riverside Church. This service assisted women in obtaining abortions when abortion was still prohibited by the criminal code. The Clergy Consultation Service concept spread throughout the country and became part of a larger movement of civil disobedience to restrictive abortion laws. Dr. Bernard Nathanson, who presided over thousands of abortions, legal and illegal, as head of a New York City abortion clinic, was a prominent physician who worked with the Clergy Consultation Service in defying the law in New York State in order to perform safe abortions.[7]

Beginning in the late 1960s, pro-abortion activism became particularly fashionable among affluent upper middle class matrons who ascribed to an almost utopian vision that abortion on demand would solve many social problems by eliminating unwanted children. In some cases, claims were made that abortion on demand would greatly reduce child abuse, juvenile delinquency, mental illness, and dependency on welfare. Moreover, the bureaucratic governing elites in certain mainline Protestant churches with traditions of social activism presented abortion rights as merely a logical extension of their church's commitment to equal rights for women. Through their superior knowledge of internal church politics, these same elites were often successful in imposing an endorsement of abortion on demand as their church's official position in site of substantial disagreement at the grass roots level. In contrast, other groups viewed the legalization of abortion as part of an insidious assault on traditional values. This paper will analyze the positions taken on abortion by several prominent American religious groups. It will focus on divisions within the Catholic, Wesleyan, Lutheran, Reformed, Anglican, Jewish, and Baptist traditions.

I. The Catholic Tradition

The abortion controversy has become a divisive factor among Catholics and Protestants, because a prominent tactic of the pro-abortionists has been to brand abortion as a Catholic issue, i.e., an attempt by the Catholic hierarchy to impose Catholic doctrine upon non-Catholics. There has even been an absurd legal argument derived from this fallacious premise along the lines of the following syllogism:

Major Premise: The First Amendment establishment clause prohibits enactment of laws incorporating religious doctrines peculiar to particular denominations.
Minor Premise: Opposition to abortion is a peculiarly Catholic position.
Conclusion: Attempts to restrict abortion violate the First Amendment's establishment clause.

Even within the Catholic community, however, there has not been unanimity on the issue of abortion. Many prominent Catholic politicians have consistently supported the extension of abortion rights. For example, Rev. Robert Drinan, S.J., while serving as the sole member of the Catholic clergy in Congress, consistently voted the pro-abortion position. Senator Daniel Patrick Moynihan even received an award from a major pro-abortion group for his efforts on behalf of the cause, and the only Catholic on the Supreme Court, Justice Brennan, has consistently voted the pro-abortion position. Catholic politicians have often taken a pro-abortion stance publicly while indicating personal opposition to abortion.

On the other hand, at the hierarchical level, the Catholic bishops have consistently opposed liberalized abortion laws. The fundamental principle underlying the Catholic Church's approach to abortion was recalled by the Second Vatican Council:

> For God, the Lord of Life, has conferred on men the surpassing ministry of safeguarding life—a ministry which must be fulfilled in a manner worthy of man. Therefore, from the moment of conception life must be guarded with the greatest of care, while abortion and infanticide are unspeakable crimes.[8]

The National Conference of Catholic Bishops has stated that they consider the passage of a pro-life constitutional amendment "a priority of the highest order."[9] Furthermore, the American bishops have declared that "the opinion of the Court [in *Roe v. Wade*] is wrong and entirely contrary to the fundamental principles of morality."[10] Pastoral guidelines prohibit Catholic hospitals from providing abortion services and Catholics from taking part in such procedures.[11] The new code of canon law retains participation in abortion as grounds for automatic excommunication which has traditionally included the woman who obtained the abortion, the doctor who performed the abortion, the person who persuaded the woman to have the abortion, and any person who cooperated to the extent that the abortion would not otherwise have taken place without his or her cooperation. Since excommunication is a special penalty, the conditions under which it applies are strictly construed, and generally it does not apply to nurses assisting at an abortion and legislators voting for liberalized abortion.[12]

In testifying before Congress in 1974, Cardinal John Krol, archbishop of Philadelphia, even refused to endorse a life of the mother exception as part of a proposed constitutional amendment proscribing abortion.[13] This is in line with the traditional Catholic stance on abortion, which does not recognize a life of the mother exception but does allow indirect abortion as opposed to direct abortion. The typical examples of the former are the ectopic pregnancy and the removal of a cancerous womb.

Subsequently, however, the bishops have become more pragmatic in their approach to abortion and have supported the proposed Hatch Amendment, a state's rights approach which would give the states and the federal government the right to proscribe abortion within their respective domains.[14]

The traditional Catholic position opposing abortion has also been the basis of extensive activity by Catholic lay persons in the National Right to Life Committee, its various state affiliates, and other anti-abortion groups such as Americans United for Life.

Unfortunately, however, the traditional Catholic position on abortion has also often been misrepresented by both Catholic and Protestant abortion proponents. This confusion results from a misunderstanding of the Church's position on ensoulment. Typically, abortion proponents suggest that the Church's position proscribing all abortions is a relatively recent development by pointing to Aquinas's theories that the human embryo, as it developed, went through vegetative, animal, and human phases. On this basis, Aquinas theorized that the time of ensoulment was forty days for the male embryo and eighty days for the female embryo. On this authority the Church developed differing punishments for abortion depending on the state of fetal development. This distinction was later picked up by the

Common Law, which punished abortion as homicide only if performed after quickening.[15]

On the other hand, the Catholic Church has always regarded participation in any abortion, regardless of stage of fetal development, as a very grave sin.[16] Moreover, with modern scientific data available on fetal development, Aquinas's theory as a basis for differing punishments has been discarded. Nevertheless, abortion proponents consistently use Aquinas's theory to argue that the Catholic Church initially did not condemn abortions performed prior to quickening.

Although the Catholic Church has consistently condemned abortion and provided leadership in the anti-abortion movement, its position is not peculiarly Catholic. Rather, the Catholic position is based on natural law and a commitment to human rights that goes beyond religious categories. It is based on the recognition of the sacredness of all human life from the time of conception: a proposition recognized by many Protestants, Jews, Hindus, Buddhists, Muslims, agnostics, and atheists.

In opposition to the traditional Catholic position are the activities of "Catholics for a Free Choice." This New York-based group was formed to support the Supreme Court's decision in *Roe v. Wade*. Its formation was announced in 1973 by Pat Fogarty McQuillan at a press conference at the NARAL Convention.[17] A militant feminist orientation has led to shrill attacks on the Church's hierarchy:

The Catholic Church's all-male celibate hierarchy still maintains an oppressive discriminatory and sexist code of laws regarding women, which have not yet been successfully challenged, while at the same time it forbids women any representation on their own behalf on the policy-making and canonical, interpretative bodies. Sinful and barbaric laws forbidding women their human, personal right to terminate an unwanted and impossible conception, were forced upon them, in and out of marriage, and deprived them of their human and inalienable right to their own souls, conscience, free will and full womanhood, reducing them to the unholy status of bondage and slavery to a patriarchal mystique which insisted on the state and male ownership of every woman's body and mind.[18]

This group has also distorted the historic position of the Church by asserting that until 1869, except for a brief interlude from 1588 to 1591, the Church condoned abortion within up to forty days for males and eighty days for female fetuses.[19]

II. The Wesleyan Tradition

The Wesleyan tradition includes the United Methodist Church, the Free Methodists, and various holiness churches, both Pentecostal and non-Pentecostal. The common religious tradition of this group traces back to John Wesley and his emphasis on personal holiness through the experience of sanctification.

The United Methodist Church, the largest in the Wesleyan tradition, has been in the forefront of pro-abortion activities since the late 1960s. Although many Methodists personally oppose abortion, the social principles of the Methodist Church adopted in 1972 favor abortion on demand:

Our belief in the sanctity of unborn human life makes us reluctant to approve abortion. But we are equally bound to respect the sacredness of the life and wellbeing of the mother, for whom devastating damage may result from an unacceptable pregnancy. In continuity with past Christian teaching, we recognize conflicts of life with life that may justify abortion. We call all Christians into a searching and prayerful inquiry into the source of conditions that may warrant abortion. We support the removal of abortion from the criminal code, placing it instead under laws relating to other procedures of standard medical practice. A decision concerning abortion should be made after thorough and thoughtful consideration by the parties involved, with medical and pastoral counsel.[20]

The Methodist position thus contains a stark contradiction. While recognizing the sanctity of unborn life, it advocates abortion on demand. In terms of moral theology, it merely admonishes resort to prayer before obtaining an abortion; it does not provide specific guidance to individual Christians contemplating the abortion decision. Without objective guidelines any abortion decision could be rationalized as a justifiable response to immediate circumstances, whether those circumstances are life-threatening or merely inconvenient.

Moreover, the Methodist Church's reference to "past Christian teaching" is apparently based upon a misconception concerning the Catholic position on ensoulment. In justifying the official position, its chief proponent, Methodist Bishop James Armstrong, used the historic debate over the time of ensoulment to argue that "it was not until 1869 that the Catholic Church decided that the embryo is ensouled at the moment of conception and that abortion at any time is the equivalent of murder."[21] Bishop Armstrong stated: "Now we are being asked to write the views of that religious congregation into the laws of the land. This is not what our forefathers envisioned as they defined a wall of separation between church and state."[22]

Although Bishop Armstrong's testimony is technically correct, the official statement is misleading, because the Church has always considered direct abortion to be morally wrong whatever the stage of fetal development. The Catholic Church has, admittedly, sometimes limited its penalties to abortions occurring after the estimated time of ensoulment. In 1869, however, Pius IX eliminated this distinction from canon law, and henceforth all direct abortions occurring after conception were penalized with excommunication.[23]

Several prominent Methodist theologians have dissented from the church's official position. Dr. Albert Outler, a professor at the Perkins School of Theology in Dallas, Texas, has stated:

> As a loyal and devoted United Methodist, I can say with great emphasis that the current "official" position of the United Methodist Church regarding abortion not only does not speak for me but that I regard the process by which this "position" became "official" as being non-representative and morally invalid.[24]

Another Methodist theologian who has expressed opposition to abortion is Paul Ramsey, a professor in the Department of Religion of Princeton University. Professor Ramsey has expressed concern that the United Methodist Church's Board of Christian Social Concern has attempted to turn the abortion issue, which he views as a human rights issue, into a church-state issue, i.e., Catholics vs. mainline Protestants. Professor Ramsey further notes that in supporting permissive abortion, "they [the Board of Christian Social Concern] depart from the entirety of the Christian tradition until now . . . and they do so . . . without proof from either scripture or sound reason."[25] Professor Ramsey emphasizes that expressions of opinion by the General Conference do not represent the considered opinions of grass roots Methodists throughout the nation. The Conference, which meets only every four years for only two weeks, is not in any sense a deliberative body. It speaks to issues after only abbreviated debate and typically passes on positions prepared in advance by various Boards which are self-perpetuating bureaucracies.[26]

Methodist theologian, J. Robert Nelson, Dean of the Boston University School of Theology, has commented on the reason for the stark contradiction in the Methodist statement as adopted in 1972 at the Atlanta Conference:

> "The legislative history" of that statement was that the call for removing abortion from the criminal code was an amendment hurriedly introduced in too brief debate in Atlanta. Hence, the contradiction of moral outlooks between

that call and the meaning of the language according human life to the unborn, with all that implies.[27]

In contrast to the United Methodist position, the other churches in the Wesleyan tradition almost uniformly condemn abortion except in very limited circumstances. The two oldest black churches, the African Methodist Episcopal Church and the African Methodist Episcopal Zion Church, condemn abortion except where the life of the mother is at stake. The Assemblies of God, the largest Pentecostal denomination, condemns abortion as morally wrong when used for socio-economic reasons. Abortion is approved by the Assemblies only where necessary to safeguard the life or health of the mother and perhaps in rape or incest cases after careful counseling. The National Association of Evangelicals, of which the Assemblies is the largest member, takes a virtually identical stance. Most other Pentecostal churches, including the United Pentecostal Church, the Pentecostal Holiness, the Foursquare, and the Church of God (Cleveland, Tennessee) have taken even stronger anti-abortion stands. The members of non-Pentecostal holiness churches such as the Nazarene and Free Methodists are also typically anti-abortion.[28]

III. Lutherans

In the disputation *De Homine,* Martin Luther indicated his belief in the full humanity of the fetus from the time of conception. Although Martin Luther himself condemned abortion, the three largest Lutheran bodies in the United States are divided on this question. The Lutheran Church in America has officially supported abortion on demand, the American Lutheran's position is unclear, and the Missouri Synod has generally opposed abortion on demand.

In the summer of 1970, the Lutheran Church in America adopted the following statement:

> Since the fetus is the organic beginning of human life, the termination of its development is always a serious matter.

Nevertheless, a qualitative distinction must be made between its claims and the rights of a responsible person made in God's image who is in living relationship with God and other human beings. This understanding of responsible personhood is congruent with the historic Lutheran teaching and practice whereby only living persons are baptized.

On the basis of the evangelical ethic, a woman or couple may decide responsibly to seek an abortion. Earnest consideration should be given to the life and total health of the mother, her responsibilities to others in the family, the state of development of the fetus, the economic and psychological stability of the home, the law of the land, and the consequences for society as a whole.[29]

The Lutheran Church in America's statement is contradictory insofar as it acknowledges that the fetus is a human being in the biological sense, but seeks to deny it dignity in the social sense. Its purported evangelical ethic amounts to an ethic of abortion on demand as a solution for social problems. While setting forth a number of factors that a Christian should consider prior to obtaining an abortion, it ultimately endorses the concept that abortion is a private choice which should be free of social controls or legal parameters. Finally, the reference to baptism is puzzling: there is no apparent connection between the practice of baptizing only living persons and the endorsement of abortion on demand.

Another major Lutheran body, the American Lutheran Church (ALC), has avoided taking a definitive denominational stand on the abortion question. In 1952, the Church took the position that "abortion must be regarded as the destruction of a living being, and except as a medical measure to save the mother's life, will not be used by a Christian to avoid unwanted birth."[30] In 1966, however, the Church allowed that "there are times and circumstances when interruption to a pregnancy may be necessary for therapeutic reasons."[31] Subsequently, an effort to win acceptance of abortion by the Commission of Research and Social Action of the ALC was turned back in 1970.[32] In

1980, the American Lutheran Church's annual convention adopted two statements on abortion seemingly contradictory in content. The first statement, based on material from the standing committee of the Office of Research and Analysis and recommended by the Executive Committee of the Church Council, took a stronger stand against abortion than the second statement, which was submitted by a 14-member task force established at the request of the 1978 general convention.

The statement recommended by the Church Council was adopted by a 609-323 vote as a statement of "judgment and conviction."[33] It deplored "the alarming increase of induced abortions since the 1973 Supreme Court decision,"[34] rejected abortion "for personally convenient or selfish reasons,"[35] and "deplored the absence of any legal protection for human life from the time of conception to birth."[36] But the statement further acknowledged that "there may be circumstances when, all pertinent factors responsibly considered, an induced abortion may be a tragic option."[37]

The 1980 convention also accepted on a 618-274 vote the task force's report as a statement of "comment and counsel."[38] This second statement, adopted "as information, as one expression of views to be considered by member congregations of the ALC,"[39] deplored "the tendency to turn to abortion as a quick and easy solution to an unplanned or a problem pregnancy."[40] It also, however, distinguished between potential personhood and actual personhood, concluding that "the interests of women are paramount where abortion is concerned."[41]

Perhaps the clearest test of ALC grass roots sentiment on the abortion question came in the 1972 North Dakota abortion referendum. In that state, where the ALC is the largest single church, a 78 percent vote was cast against a proposed liberalized abortion law.[42]

Unlike the other two major Lutheran bodies in the United States, the Lutheran Church-Missouri Synod has taken a stand against abortion on demand. One lay woman, representing the Church and appearing on behalf of its Board for Social Concern, criticized abortion on demand as offering "death as a solution to economic and social problems," thereby doing "violence to the integrity of women."[43] The Missouri Synod has also officially expressed opposition to abortion through a denominational statement of its 1971 National Convention and a document produced by its Commission on Theology and Church Relations.

According to its official denominational statement, the Missouri Synod regards willful abortion as contrary to the will of God. Elaborating on this statement, the Report of the Commission of Theological and Church Relations[44] regards all non-therapeutic abortions as wrong, defining therapeutic abortions as those done to "safeguard the health or life of the patient, or to prevent the birth of a severely crippled, deformed, or abnormal infant."[45] The Report approached the abortion issue from theological, medical, and legal perspectives, and there are certain discrepancies among these various perspectives.

In its treatment of theological aspects of the abortion issue, the Report set out four basic guiding principles: (1) life is a gift from God; (2) human beings are created for eternal life; (3) human life is created for fulfillment; and (4) life and death belong to the province of God. The Report accepted the implantation of the blastocyst, which occurs approximately one week after fertilization, as the beginning of individual human life. In case of a conflict between the nascent life and the life of the mother, the Report indicated the life of the mother takes precedence. The Report did not explicitly rule out abortion in cases of rape and incest, but did indicate these are "special problems requiring pastoral counseling of the most sensitive kind."[46] The existence of very grave psychiatric considerations were not deemed in and of themselves to provide a justification for abortion. Finally, the Report acknowledged that life comes into being as a special creative act of God and that no gift of God can be rejected or destroyed with impunity.

With respect to legal aspects, the Report expresses hope that the laws will respect the teaching of holy scripture on the abortion question. The specific scriptural references found in the Report's treatment of theological aspects were:

(1) Exodus 21:22-24, where the law of retaliation is made to apply in cases of injury to a mother or child in her womb or to both.

(2) Jeremiah 1:5, which speaks of the consecration of a prophet before he was born; and

(3) Luke 1:41, describing how the unborn baby in Elizabeth's womb leaped for joy at Mary's greeting.[47]

These scriptural passages are deemed to establish that life in the womb is indeed an individual human life. The approach to bringing the law into conformity with this scriptural insight is somewhat cautious. The Report acknowledged the difficulty of enforcing a law where the principal surviving support for the law was the religious credo of a minority or diminishing majority. In this case, it concluded, regretfully, that the "law has lost its title to public authority."[48] On the other hand, it asserted the legalization of abortion in no way dispensed the Christian from the obligation to conform to the higher law of the Gospel.

With respect to medical aspects, the Report concluded that the Christian physician can, in some circumstances, e.g., when the life of the mother is threatened by the pregnancy, accept and actually recommend abortion. Finally, the Report suggested that although holy scripture does not contain a detailed set of regulations on abortion, it does set forth enduring principles which give the Christian a basis for making personal choices on the abortion question.[49]

IV. The Reformed Tradition

John Calvin stated: "If some woman expels the fetus from her uterus with drugs, it is considered an inexplicable crime and rightly so."[50] Another statement by Calvin made clear his position: "The fetus carried in the mother's womb is already a man; and it is quite unnatural that a life be destroyed of one who has not yet seen its enjoyment."[51]

In contrast, some churches in the Reformed tradition have in recent years endorsed abortion on demand. In 1970, the General Assemblies of both the Presbyterian Church in the United States[52] and the United Presbyterian Church,[53] the two largest Presbyterian bodies, adopted statements supporting reform of abortion laws, and the United Presbyterian Women adopted a resolution supporting abortion on demand.[54]

A basic premise of the 1970 General Assembly statement of the Presbyterian Church in the United States was that in order to not overpopulate the world, it is necessary to "interfere in the life process."[55] This statement began by acknowledging that abortion has historically been widely regarded as a serious offense. The statement also acknowledged that Roman Catholics have always regarded willful abortion as a serious sin, regardless of the stage of fetal development. The statement then set out several biblical and theological insights acknowledging that biblical faith, while demanding "profound respect for human life," also called us to improve the "quality of life." The statement asserted that the abortion decision is a private choice. It cautioned that while the rights of the fetus should be respected, the needs of the mother, her family, and society may at times take precedence over the rights of the fetus. Accordingly, the statement acknowledged that abortion may on occasion be morally justifiable. The possible justifying circumstances enumerated were medical indications of physical or mental deformity, conception as a result of rape or incest, conditions under which the physical or mental health of either mother or child would be gravely threatened, or possible adverse effects on the socioeconomic condition of the family. The statement emphasized the hard cases and in this regard stopped somewhat short of approving abortion for its members in all cases. The 1970 statement concluded that "(l)aws concerning abortion should reflect principles set forth in this paper."[56]

In its 1972 General Assembly the United Presbyterian Church adopted a resolution supporting full freedom of personal choice for women on the abortion decision, easily available low-cost abortion services, and the repeal of restrictive abortion laws.[57] The 1972 resolution elaborated on a 1970 resolution calling for repeal of all abortion laws.

The basis for the 1972 resolution was a report produced, pursuant to the recommendations of the 1970 General Assembly, by a committee that consisted of five women and four men. This report repeated the erroneous charge that the Catholic position prohibiting early abortions did not emerge until 1869, and in support thereof refers to various views on the question of when ensoulment occurs.

The report identified three possible positions concerning abortion:

(1) Abortion should be permitted only when the mother's life is in danger. The report erroneously notes this is the Roman Catholic position, as well as the position of the 1962 General Assembly Committee on Responsible Marriage and Parenthood.

(2) Abortion should be available on demand during the first trimester but should be restricted in later phases of pregnancy. The report notes this was the position taken by the American Law Institute in 1967.

(3) Abortion should be permitted at any stage. Justification of this position is based on the bodily rights of a woman and the assumption a person does not exist until after birth.[58]

The report then ridiculed the first position as based on unsubstantiated speculation as to the time of ensoulment and an antiquated negative attitude towards human sexuality. The second alternative was also quickly dismissed because it perpetuated "the assumption that abortion is justifiable homicide," and does not "deal with the problem of bodily rights of the woman, and does not grant her the right not to bear an unwanted child."[59] Ultimately only the third position was found acceptable by the report.

Finally, the report urged support of all Christians for such agencies as Planned Parenthood and the Clergy Consultation Service in their battle for unrestricted free abortions. Somewhat mysteriously, however, in view of the report's conclusion, the committee indicated some discomfort with the use of abortion as a means of limiting family size.[60]

Another mainline Protestant body with its roots in the Reformed tradition is the United Church of Christ, which was formed in June 1957 by the union of the Evangelical and Reformed Church and the General Council of the Congregational Churches of the United States. As late as 1960, the Council for Christian Social Action, an agency of the United Church, declared that "Christian conscience cannot approve of abortion as a means of family planning, for it violates personality and involves the destruction of human life."[61] Subsequently, however, many of the Church's clergy were involved in the Clergy Consultation Service on Problem Pregnancies.

In 1960, a disagreement on abortion developed within the Church. The Church Board for Homeland Ministries adopted a statement supporting repeal of all restrictive abortion laws.[62] Another Church agency, the Council for Christian Social Action, supported removal of restriction only during the early months of pregnancy.[63]

Pursuant to the standard church policy, at the Eighth General Synod, held in June 1971, the Committee on Pronouncements reported that a poll of local churches, delegates, conferences, associations, and other individuals, indicated overwhelming support for removal of restrictions on abortion during the early months. A delegate then moved to adopt a substitute proposal calling for removal of all restrictions on abortion, regardless of stage of pregnancy. Eventually, a statement supporting abortion on demand was adopted at the 1971 General Synod. The resolution stated that if constitutional amendments were adopted which restricted abortion, they would conflict with the establishment clause of the First Amendment. The statement polemically noted "if the Government said a woman had to give birth to a fetus, without regard to any and all circumstances, that dictation would reduce her personhood to that of an animal and constitute a gross violation of our Christian faith."[64]

Rev. Albert W. Kovacs, an ordained Church of Christ minister and pro-life activist, strongly condemned the method by which the pro-abortion position of the United Church of Christ was formulated. Kovacs contended the two proposals were tardily released by the denomination and, accordingly, no serious dialogue ever took place. Kovacs continued, "(t)he total ignorance of theological implications was appalling for a church body," and the Church seemed to be "weighing the value of life in dollars and cents or in opposition to Catholics."[65]

VI. *Judaism*

Judaism, like Christianity, is also split on the abortion question. Reform Judaism has actively championed the cause of abortion on demand while Orthodox Judaism accepts abortion only when necessary to save the life of the mother. Reform scholars have based their refusal to consider abortion as murder on Exodus 21:22:

> If men strive and hurt a pregnant woman so that her fruit be expelled, but no harm befall her, then shall he be fined as her husband shall assess, and the matter placed before the judges. But if harm befall her, then thou shalt give life for life.[66]

Reform scholars have interpreted this passage to show that only monetary compensation is exacted of him who causes a woman to miscarry. Reform scholars have also relied on a reference to embryotomy found in the Mishnah, an ancient code of Jewish law which formed the basis of the Talmud:

> [In the case of a] woman who is having difficulty in giving birth, it is permitted to cut up the child inside her womb and

take it out limb by limb because her life takes precedent. However, if the greater part of the child has come out, it must not be touched because one life must not be taken to save another.[67]

On the basis of these sources and the absence of an explicit condemnation of abortion, most Reform scholars have concluded that Jewish Law does not consider abortion to be murder. A basic underlying premise of this position is that the fetus is not a person and therefore not entitled to legal protection. Reform scholars also have emphasized the woman's freedom of choice with regard to abortion and the necessity of limiting population growth.

In light of these arguments, the National Council of Jewish Women, the National Federation of Temple Sisterhoods, the B'nai B'rith Women, and the American Union of Hebrew Congregations have become members of the Religious Coalition for Abortion Rights.[68]

On the other hand, Orthodox authorities have traditionally viewed abortion as one of the "abominations of Egypt" which the Torah was intended to eliminate.[69]

Relying on the statement from the Mishnah permitting embryotomy, most Orthodox scholars have inferred that destruction of the fetus is prohibited in instances not involving a threat to the life of the pregnant mother. Furthermore, the inference that has been derived from Exodus 21:22 by many Orthodox rabbis is that although feticide is not a capital offense, the fetus is, nevertheless, sufficiently human to render its destruction a moral offense.[70]

There has been, however, uncertainty in Orthodox circles as to when a fetus gains human life. Some have held a fetus attains human life from the moment of conception, others that human life is attained at forty days after conception, and still others that it is not attained until three months after conception. Nevertheless, most Orthodox scholars have prohibited abortion from the time of conception except where necessary to save the mother's life on the basis of the obligation under the Sinaitic covenant to be fruitful and multiply and the further prohibition against destroying the seed (semen).[71]

Virtually all Orthodox authorities have viewed the Mishnah passage on permitting embryotomy as mandating that the life of the fetus is subordinate to that of the mother prior to birth. On the other hand, interference with natural process after the moment of birth has been prohibited, birth being defined as the emergence of the forehead or the greater part thereof from the womb. The underlying rationale for this position is that until the moment of birth the child is viewed as an aggressor pursuing the life of the mother, but once birth has occurred, heaven is the pursuer. Some authorities have held that the underlying law of pursuit cannot be invoked in cases of doubt. Accordingly, abortion has been permitted only when there is incontrovertible medical evidence that the pregnancy per se would result in the death of the mother.[72]

Some authorities have also held that Noachides (those under the covenant of Noah) are specifically enjoined from destroying fetal life on the basis of Genesis 9:6: "Whoever sheds the blood of man, by man shall his blood be shed." Consequently, any aid extended by a Jew to a Gentile in the performance of an abortion has been viewed as contrary to Leviticus 19:14: "Thou shalt not put a stumbling block before the blind" (Lv 19:14). Furthermore, some authorities have held it is not even clear that a Noachide may destroy the life of a fetus in order to save the mother's life.[73]

Other Orthodox authorities have held that there is a fundamental distinction between Jewish Law and the Noachidic Law with respect to the assessment of potential life. According to many authorities, Noachides, unlike Jews, are not obligated to preserve the lives of their fellows, to "be fruitful and multiply," or to refrain from wasting the male seed. Accordingly, while Noachides are forbidden to commit homicide, they are under no responsibility to safeguard seminal life. Under this view, there has been no objection to Noachides aborting or to a Jew giving advice and rendering indirect assistance to Noachides in aborting a fetus within the first forty days of gestation, because during this period the fetus has not developed sufficiently for its destruction to constitute homicide.[74] Moreover, the absence in the Noachidic code of a ban on feticide during the first forty days of gestation provides an insight into what has often been considered an erroneous translation in the Septuagint version of Exodus 21:22-23:

> And if two men strive and smite a woman with child, and her child be born imperfectly formed, he shall be forced to pay a penalty. . . . But if it be perfectly formed, he shall give life for life.

This passage has been interpreted as requiring the death penalty only for the killing of a formed fetus, i.e., one having reached its fortieth day of gestation.[75] One rabbinic tradition has speculated that this modification in the Septuagint was intentionally introduced by Jewish translators; i.e., since the Septuagint was addressed to Gentiles, the translation may have been intended to incorporate ramifications of Noachidic Law.[76] At any rate, this rendering of Exodus 21:22-23 did influence the Roman Catholic Church's assessment of penalties for early abortion.[77]

Finally, during Senate Committee hearings on a constitutional amendment proscribing abortion, Rabbi David Bleich, as a representative of the Rabbinical Council of America, endorsed an amendment prohibiting abortion except where necessary to save the life of the mother.[78] In answer to an inquiry from Senator Fong as to whether this would improperly impose a sectarian doctrine, Rabbi Bleich stated:

> I would view feticide as a form of manslaughter as such fetal life is entitled to protection just as full-fledged human life is entitled to protection. And society, in doing that, is simply reflecting moral views, which are not part of the sectarian code of any specific religious denomination but rather a part of the common morality of Western Civilization.[79]

VII. The Baptists

Baptists, with the exception of the American Baptists, are usually biblical conservatives and therefore strongly pro-life. Baptists for Life was formed in 1973 to speak in defense of the right to life. It has received positive responses in large numbers of Southern Baptists, American Baptists, Independent Baptists, and other denominational groupings, including the largest Black Baptist group, the National Baptist Convention.[80]

Since Baptist groups are usually organized on a congregational basis, it has been difficult for them to express a unified position on abortion. Like-minded congregations, however, typically meet together at an annual meeting or convention, and several of these conventions have passed resolutions condemning abortion which, although not binding on individual members, at least have expressed the opinion of a majority of those present at the convention.[81]

In 1971, the Annual Southern Baptist Convention, the largest Baptist group, adopted a resolution calling upon Southern Baptists to work for legislation allowing abortion only in cases of rape, incest, clear evidence of severe fetal deformity, and carefully ascertained evidence of the likelihood of damage to the emotional, mental, and physical health of the mother.[82] Subsequently, however, in 1980 the Annual Southern Baptist Convention passed a resolution expressing support for a constitutional amendment prohibiting abortion except when necessary to save the life of the mother.[83]

On the other hand, the American Baptist Churches in the U.S.A., the major Northern Baptist body, has been in the forefront of efforts to legalize abortion and is a member of the RCAR. In 1968, the American Baptist Convention expressed approval of abortion legislation resembling the American Law Institute's Model Penal Code. The American Baptists have also resorted to unfortunate nativist tactics in the hope of thwarting attempts to restrict abortion by labelling it as a Catholic issue. In 1974, the American Baptist's Committee on Christian Unity submitted a paper to the U.S. Senate Subcommittee on Constitutional Amendments which expressed criticism of the efforts of Catholics to enact a constitutional amendment restricting abortion:

> . . . (W)e believe that the present national effort of the National Conference of Catholic Bishops in the U.S.A. to coerce the conscience and personal freedom of our citizens through the power of public law in matters of human reproduction constitutes a serious threat to the moral and religious liberty so highly prized by Baptists and so long protected for all people under the nation's policy of the separation of Church and State.[84]

VIII. The Anglican Tradition

In the 1930 Lambeth Conference, the Bishops of the Church of England approved contraception but also condemned "the sinful practice of abortion."[85] In 1958, the Lambeth Conference reiterated: "In the strongest terms, Christians reject the practice of induced abortion, or infanticide, which involves the killing of a life already conceived."[86] Subsequently, the 1968 Lambeth Conference reaffirmed the 1958 resolution.[87]

In contrast, at its 62nd General Convention held in Seattle in 1967, the Protestant Episcopal Church in the United States deviated sharply from the traditional Anglican position on abortion. It adopted a resolution supporting abortion where "the physical or mental health of the mother is threatened seriously, or where there is substantial reason to believe that the child would be badly deformed in mind or body, or where the pregnancy has resulted from rape or incest."[88]

In 1976, at the 65th General Convention held in Minneapolis, the 1967 position was reaffirmed.[89] The 1976 Convention also urged seeking the counsel of a priest of the Church where abortion was sought for reasons other than those specified in the 1967 resolution, expressed opposition to abortion for birth control purposes, and expressed "unequivocal opposition" to any legislation restricting abortion.[90] In spite of the Episcopal Church's position, its Executive Committee has rejected attempts to enlist it as a member of the Religious Coalition for Abortion Rights.[91]

Typically, more traditionally oriented Episcopalians, particularly those influenced by the Oxford movement, have been opposed to abortion. In fact, many Anglo-Catholics left the Episcopal Church after the 1976 convention. The divergent views of two prominent Anglican moral theologians illustrate the division within the Anglican Communion over the abortion issue. Herbert Waddams has condemned the pro-abortion stance as a confused appeal to subjective aesthetic and sentimental standards.[92] On the other hand, Joseph Fletcher has stated "there ought to be no unwanted babies," and proposed abortion as a solution to socio-economic problems and a backup for contraceptive failure.[93]

Conclusion

Religious groups in the United States have taken an active political role on both sides of the abortion question. A group's position on abortion is often an indicator of that group's adherence to traditional Judeo-Christian values. In several mainline Protestant churches support of these traditional values have been subordinated in recent years to other values emphasizing self-fulfillment and self-gratification, and a commitment to feminist causes. Indeed, abortion is a litmus test issue, because a group that supports abortion may also depart from Judeo-Christian tradition in other matters concerning human sexuality, such as sexual preference and sex outside of marriage. Although religious groups have played an important part in the abortion controversy, abortion is not a religious issue in sectarian terms. Abortion proponents and abortion opponents may be found in all major creeds and confessions. For example, in the Rocky Mountain West, abortion is often viewed as a Mormon issue because of the Mormons' opposition to abortion except under very limited circumstances. Orthodox Jews, fundamentalist Christians, Muslims, Buddhists, and Hindus typically oppose abortion on demand. On the other hand, many Catholic politicians and lay people have publicly supported abortion on demand in contravention of their church's teaching.

Ultimately, abortion is a human rights issue which cuts across religious categories. A society's regard for human dignity is indicated by its willingness to protect innocent human life. One particularly worrisome trend is the attempt by an intellectual and professional elite to define human life in social terms. The Nazi experience certainly demonstrates the perils of this approach: the extermination policies of Nazi Germany were not, as popularly believed, imposed from above by Nazi ideologues. Rather, the genesis of these policies came from academic and professional groups. For example, it was the German psychiatric profession which first proposed the extermination of the mentally ill. With the support of German psychiatrists and other medical professionals, the policy of eliminating "useless eaters" was later extended to the elderly, disabled veterans, and even children who happened to become burdens on the state. The extermination techniques used in these programs were later adopted by special death squads (Einsatzgruppen) composed of S.S. members, Protestant pastors, and lawyers. In addition, the German medical profession utilized inmates of concentration camps as subjects of otherwise impermissible, painful, and deadly experiments on live human beings. Thus the professions of law, medicine, and theology contributed to the creation of a moral and intellectual climate where human lives were assessed only in utilitarian terms.

Two aspects of the religiously motivated pro-abortion movement have been particularly disturbing: its attempts to stir up religious bigotry and its failure to acknowledge the higher calling of the gospel. A prominent tactic of the pro-abortion movement has been to portray the pro-life movement as merely a tool of the Catholic bishops. Unfortunately, appeals to nativist sympathies have been frequently resorted to by the leaders of certain mainline Protestant denominations in order to gather support for abortion on demand. These same denominations in their official position statements on abortion have typically failed to distinguish between morality and legality. By endorsing abortion on demand as a desirable social policy, they have failed to acknowledge the greater demands of the gospel on the individual Christian. Even if it is conceded that there is no longer a sufficient consensus to support laws restricting abortion, this should not dispense the churches from requiring a higher standard of behavior of their members, and generally supporting efforts to curtail abortions.

FOUR

Amniocentesis, Coercion, and Privacy

Charles E. Rice

T HE 1973 ABORTION DECISIONS of the Supreme Court were
based on a right of reproductive privacy which the Court
in 1965 had discovered in certain elusive "penumbras formed
by emanations from the Bill of Rights."[1] This fictional right of
privacy was used by the Court to declare unconstitutional
virtually all state restrictions on abortion; according to the
Court's rulings, the states have no effective power to prohibit
abortion at any stage of pregnancy. Even in the third trimester,
the state may not prohibit abortion where it is necessary "in
appropriate medical judgment for the preservation of the life or
health of the mother."[2] Since the Court defined the health of
the mother to include "psychological as well as physical well-
being" and said that "the medical judgment may be exercised in
the light of all factors—physical, emotional, psychological,
familial, and the woman's age—relevant to the well-being of the
mother,"[3] the ruling is a license for elective abortion at every
stage of pregnancy up to the time of normal delivery.

One widely overlooked aspect of *Roe v. Wade*, however, is its
implicit sanction of compulsory abortion. As Professor Robert
Byrn noted in his definitive article on the decision:

It must be remembered that the Court in Wade rejected

any absolute right of a woman to choose whether or not to abort, and premised its holding on a limited right of privacy, subordinate to compelling state interests. As one example of an appropriate state limitation on the right of privacy, the court cited *Buck v. Bell* (274 U.S. 200 [1927]) which upheld the validity of a state statute providing for compulsory sterilization of mental defectives whose affliction is hereditary. The state "interest" in that situation was, of course, in preventing the proliferation of defectives.

It had been thought that *Buck v. Bell* died after the Nazi experience, and its revival now is rather frightening. By implication in Wade, the Court espoused the constitutional validity of state-imposed, compulsory abortion of unborn children diagnosed intrautero as mentally defective. Neither the child's constitutional rights (of which the Court could find none) nor the mother's right of privacy (which the Court, by citing Buck, found limited by the state's "interest" in preventing the birth of mental defectives) could, according to the theory of Wade, be interposed to challenge such a statute.[4]

Fortunately, in the decade since *Roe v. Wade,* the courts have not explicitly recognized the legitimacy of compulsory abortion. However, technological developments have recently established the foundation for a compulsory eugenics program:

During the past decade, advances in the antenatal diagnosis of genetic disorders have proceeded at a revolutionary pace. Amniocentesis and karyo-type analysis of fetal cells have made the detection of Down's syndrome (trisomy 21) and a host of other chromosomal abnormalities almost routine. In 1979, 28.7% of all pregnant women in New York age 35 or older underwent prenatal cytogenetic studies. Steady advances in ultrasonography, fetoscopy, biochemical screening, and the application of recombinant DNA technology to fetal DNA promise that this diagnostic revolution will not soon subside. The advent of antenatal diagnosis and the rapid growth of university-based clinics that specialize in genetic counseling have created a complicated liability problem for obstetricians, pediatricians, and family practitioners.[5]

Since 1975, courts have increasingly recognized a wrongful birth cause of action in which physicians may be held liable to parents for the costs of raising a defective child and related damages where there has been either a failure to test for defects or negligence in administering the tests.[6]

In "wrongful birth" cases parents sue for the costs of raising handicapped children. The theory of the suit is usually either that if the doctor had told them of the risks of birth defects the child would not have been conceived or that, if they had been told during the pregnancy that the child was likely to be defective, they would have had an abortion. Other "wrongful birth" cases involve the birth of normal children after a sterilization operation which failed due to the negligence of the defendant doctor.[7] This paper is not concerned with this last type of case, but rather only with cases imposing liability on doctors for negligent counseling or testing as a result of which the mother did not choose to abort her unborn child. In such cases, courts have adopted three general lines of reasoning as to the extent of damages that may be recovered:

There are cases in which courts have concluded that a physician found negligent in a "wrongful birth action" can be liable for the entire cost of raising and educating the child until the child reaches majority. While it may appear extreme, courts have held that the award of such damages is proper.

Other courts have held that while such damages are cognizable, the benefit of watching a child achieve and grow to maturity must be balanced with the cost of raising the child. The value of the benefit must be assessed to mitigate the cost of rearing the child. However, courts following either of these lines of reasoning have given no indication of what monetary amount of damages would be considered an appropriate award. Finally, some courts have rejected awarding such damages in cases involving wrongful birth actions, indicating that such damages are not cognizable, too speculative, and an unrealistic burden for the physician.[8]

For example, in *Karsons v. Guerinot*,[9] New York's intermediate appellate court allowed parents to maintain a cause of action for the birth of a mongoloid child against a physician who negligently failed to notify them of the risks of pregnancy and availability of amniocentesis. And in *Becker v. Schwartz*,[10] the highest court of New York held that a physician had a legal obligation to warn a 38-year-old woman of the increased age-related risk of bearing a child suffering from Down's syndrome. In a companion case the court recognized a cause of action on behalf of the parents of two children who had been born with a hereditary kidney disorder because after the birth of the first child the defendant doctors failed to warn them that the disease was hereditary. In both instances the *Becker* court allowed the parents to sue, but refused to permit the child to sue in its own behalf.

In addition to wrongful birth actions, the courts have recently recognized wrongful life causes of action brought on behalf of the defective child rather than the parents. The child's claim is not to recover damages for his physical or mental defect or illness which was caused or aggravated by the doctor's alleged negligence; rather it arises from maternal or genetic conditions; it is that the doctor negligently failed to discover the prospect of the child's birth defect or negligently failed to bring that prospect sufficiently to the attention of the child's parents. In order to establish causation, it is further claimed that, had the parents been properly informed of the prospect of birth defects, they would have practiced contraception or obtained an abortion so as to prevent the plaintiff's conception or birth. The essence of the claim is that the plaintiff's mere existence is a harm, and that but for the physician's breach of duty, the plaintiff would not have been born.

Initially, in *Gleitman v. Cosgrove*[11] the New Jersey Court rejected both wrongful birth and wrongful life actions. Jeffrey Gleitman was born in Jersey City on November 25, 1959, with substantial defects in sight, hearing, and speech. His mother had contracted German measles one month after she became pregnant with Jeffrey. When she was two months pregnant, she routinely consulted Drs. Cosgrove and Dolan, who practiced obstetrics and gynecology together in Jersey City. When she asked the doctors several times during the pregnancy about the effects of German measles, she "received a reassuring answer" each time. After the birth of Jeffrey, Mr. and Mrs. Gleitman sued the doctors to recover damages for the emotional effects and added financial burden caused to them by the doctors' failure to apprise them of the high risk of birth defects from German measles. The parents' theory was that, if the doctors had told them of the risks, they would have procured an abortion and thereby would have avoided their emotional and financial injury. There was no way that the birth defects could have been minimized during the pregnancy; the alternatives, therefore, were birth or abortion. More significantly, the parents sued for wrongful life on behalf of the infant Jeffrey. The court rejected by a majority vote of 4-3 all the parents' claims, on their own behalf and on behalf of Jeffrey.

In *Curlender v. Bio-Science Laboratories,*[12] however, the court recognized a wrongful life cause of action brought on behalf of a defective child against a medical laboratory which negligently administered a test to determine whether the child would be likely to be born with a genetic defect. The court stated:

We construe the wrongful-life cause of action by the defective child as the right of such child to recover damages for the pain and suffering to be endured during the limited life span available to such a child and any special pecuniary loss resulting from the impaired condition.[10]

Significantly, the court indicated that in an appropriate case the child might even be allowed to sue his own parents for allowing him to be born:

> One of the fears expressed in the decisional law is that, once it is determined that such infants have rights cognizable at law, nothing would prevent such a plaintiff from bringing suit against its own parents for allowing plaintiff to be born. In our view, the fear is groundless. The "wrongful-life" cause of action with which we are concerned is based upon negligently caused failure by someone under a duty to do so to inform the prospective parents of facts needed by them to make a conscious choice not to become parents. If a case arose where, despite due care by the medical profession in transmitting necessary warnings, parents made a conscious choice to proceed with a pregnancy, with full knowledge that a seriously impaired infant would be born, that conscious choice would provide an intervening act of proximate cause to preclude liability insofar as defendants other than the parents were concerned. Under such circumstances, we see no sound public policy which should protect those parents from being answerable for the pain, suffering and misery which they have wrought upon their offspring.[14]

No such action by the child against his own parents has been sustained, but there is some logic in the comment by Dr. Margery Shaw, acting director of the Medical Genetics Center of the University of Texas at Houston, that "it's inevitable" that such an action will be allowed. "Physicians," in Dr. Shaw's opinion, "may be required to warn patients that if they allow a defective child to be born, they may incur a liability."[15] In response to the *Curlender* court's suggestion of a potential parental liability, the California legislature enacted a statute which relieves the parents of liability in such a situation and further provides that the parents' decision shall neither be "a defense in any action against a third party" nor "be considered in awarding damages in any such action."[16]

Moreover, in *Turpin v. Sortini*, the California Supreme Court itself limited *Curlender*, holding that a child born because of a physician's wrongful failure to inform the parents of possible genetic defects could not collect damages for being allowed to exist, but could collect for the extra costs resulting from the handicap.[17] In rejecting the allowance of recovery by the child for his very existence, the court said:

The basic fallacy of the Curlender analysis is that it ignores the essential nature of the defendants' alleged wrong and obscures a critical difference between wrongful life actions and the ordinary prenatal injury cases noted above. In an ordinary prenatal injury case, if the defendant had not been negligent, the child would have been born healthy; thus, in a typical personal injury case, the defendant in such a case has interfered with the child's basic right to be free from physical injury caused by the negligence of others. In this case, by contrast, the obvious tragic fact is that plaintiff never had a chance "to be born as a whole, functional human being without total deafness"; if defendants had performed their jobs properly, she would not have been born with hearing intact, but—according to the complaint—would not have been born at all.[18]

Perhaps the most far-reaching decision in this area is *Harbeson v. Parke-Davis, Inc.,*[19] in which the Washington Supreme Court expressly recognized causes of action for wrongful birth and wrongful life. The suit was based upon medical care that Mrs. Harbeson received from military physicians who had prescribed Dilantin for her after she suffered a grand mal seizure in 1970. In March 1971, while on Dilantin, Mrs. Harbeson gave birth to a normal child. Thereafter, however, Mrs. Harbeson gave birth to two defective children who were diagnosed as suffering from fetal hydantion syndrome, i.e., they suffered from mild to moderate growth deficiencies, mild to moderate developmental retardation, wide-set eyes, lateral ptosis (drooping eyelids), hypoplasia of the fingers, small nails, low-set hairline, broad nasal ridge, and other physical and developmental defects. Prior to the conception and birth of their children, Mr. and Mrs. Harbeson had informed the military physicians that they were considering having other children and inquired about the risks of ingesting Dilantin during pregnancy. The physicians informed the Harbesons that Dilantin could cause a cleft palate and temporary hirsutism in the fetus, but they did not conduct literature searches or consult other sources for specific information regarding the correlation between Dilantin and birth defects.

Mr. and Mrs. Harbeson and a guardian ad litem appointed for the two defective children filed suit in the U.S. District Court for Western Washington and since there were no Washington cases concerning wrongful birth and wrongful life, the federal court certified several questions concerning the availability of these actions to the Washington Supreme Court.

In recognizing the existence of a wrongful birth cause of action on behalf of the parents of the defective child, the Washington Court stated:

> That this duty requires health care providers to impart to their patients material information as to the likelihood of future children being born defective, to enable the potential parent to decide whether to avoid the conception or birth of such children. The duty does not, however, affect in any way the right of a physician to refuse on moral or religious grounds to perform an abortion. Recognition of the duty will "promote societal interests in genetic counseling and prenatal testing, deter medical malpractice, and at least partially redress a clear and undeniable wrong." (Rogers, *Wrongful Life and Wrongful Birth: Medical Malpractice in Genetic Counseling and Prenatal Teaching*, 33 S.C.L. Rev. 713, 737 [1982].[20])

With respect to damages recoverable by the parents, the *Harbeson* court held that they could recover medical, hospital, and medication expenses attributable to their children's birth and defective condition, and damages for their own emotional injury. In considering damages for the parents' emotional injury, the court held that the jury would be entitled to consider the countervailing emotional benefits attributable to the child's birth.

Moreover, the *Harbeson* court held that the children could maintain a wrongful life action in order to recover the extraordinary expenses to be incurred during their lifetime as a result of the congenital defects. The court limited this recovery, however, by noting that the costs of such care during the child's minority could be recovered once, and, therefore, if the parents recovered them, the child could only recover costs incurred during majority. Finally, the *Harbeson* court denied recovery of general damages in wrongful life actions, noting that "measuring the value of an impaired life as compared to nonexistence is a task beyond that of ordinary mortals. . . ."[21]

The rise of the causes of action for wrongful birth and wrongful life is a direct outgrowth of *Roe v. Wade*. This point was recognized last year by the Seventh Circuit Court of Appeals in holding that physicians can be sued for failure to give parents the information they need to decide whether to choose abortion and that the damages can include the lifetime costs of raising the child as well as the extra costs occasioned by the child's handicap. Indeed, the court's opinion specifically recognized the routine character of the wrongful birth action once *Roe v. Wade* is accepted:

State courts have been quick to accept wrongful birth as a cause of action since *Roe v. Wade*, because it is not a significant departure from previous tort law. A case like this one is little different from an ordinary medical malpractice action. It involves a failure by a physician to meet a required standard of care, which resulted in specific damages to the plaintiffs. The government tries to separate this case from those of ordinary medical malpractice by raising political and moral questions concerning abortions, but the Supreme Court has already settled that issue. In *Roe v. Wade*, the

Court held that it was the mother's consitutional right to decide during the first trimester of pregnancy whether to obtain an abortion. The staff at the OB-GYN clinic at Fort Rucker deprived Mrs. Robak of the opportunity to make an informed decision when they failed to tell her of her rubella and the potential consequences on her fetus. Because of this negligence, the Robaks are faced with large expenses for Jennifer's care and special treatment. As in any other tort case, the defendant must bear the burden for injuries resulting from its own negligence. "Any other ruling would in effect immunize from liability those in the medical field providing inadequate guidance to persons who would choose to exercise their constitutional right to abort fetuses which, if born, would suffer from genetic (or other) defects." *Berman v. Allen, supra,* 404 A.2d at 14. The district court was therefore correct in holding that the Robaks' complaint stated a valid cause of action in wrongful birth.[22]

The well-established wrongful birth cases and the emerging wrongful life cases effectively compel doctors to inform expectant mothers of the abortion option at least in high-risk cases. Under the fear of malpractice actions, this practice may extend to all pregnancies. This trend will also force physicians to test exhaustively for any remote indication of trouble in a pregnancy and to make full disclosure of those risks to the mother. Since physicians will be virtually relieved of potential civil liability if the mother does have the abortion, the tendency will be for the doctor to emphasize that option. The compulsion is only directly applicable to the mother. Instead, it is an economic compulsion of the doctor which in turn influences his relation with the mother.

The availability of amniocentesis introduces an additional pressure on physicians to promote the choice of abortion where the test discloses fetal anomalies. Concurrently, other technological developments are making the performance of abortion a private affair known only to the woman herself (and the victim child). While the constitutional right of reproductive privacy, as invented by the Supreme Court, is essentially fictional, with no foundation in the Constitution, the New Biology is making total reproductive privacy a reality. The typical abortion of the near future will be accomplished chemically by way of pill, injection, or other method capable of self-administration. For example, a team of Swiss and French researchers has developed an after-conception pill that appears to be 100% effective in "preventing pregnancies." The woman need only take the pill for two to four days a month. It causes expulsion from the uterus of any egg fertilized that month, thus inducing an early abortion.[23] This pill, which is based on a hormone described as an anti-progesterone name RU-486, was described by *Washington Post* columnist Clayton Fritchey as "making most surgical abortions superfluous."[24] Similar products are undoubtedly in various stages of development in the United States and other countries.

Since liberalized abortion was first proposed by the American Law Institute in 1962, the right-to-life movement has concentrated on surgical abortion as the evil to be prevented. In that context, the continual debates on phrasing of a human life amendment, whether it should include exceptions and, if so, which ones, etc., were relevant. Now, however, abortion is becoming a private matter totally within the control of the mother. We have, finally, caught up with the pagan Romans who endowed the father, the paterfamilias, with the right to kill his child at his discretion, only we give that right to the mother. But it is all the same to the victim. The power of the law to control private, elective abortions will be limited. The major means of controlling such private abortions will be by licensing and regulation of the abortifacient drugs or devices.

The privatization of the abortion act and the implicit compulsion of physicians to recommend it require that the law, if it is to restore the right to life, must first reestablish the basic principle that all human beings are persons with respect to their right to life. Such a restoration will help to maintain a climate favorable to the promotion of widespread and spiritually based respect for life which is essential if private, do-it-yourself abortions are to be discouraged. The restoration of personhood to the unborn with respect to the right to life could also prevent courts from imposing liability on doctors for failing to counsel parents as to the abortion option. And, finally, the recognition of legal personhood for all human beings from the time of conception would also protect the retarded, the elderly, and others endangered by the predictable extension of the principle that some innocent human beings can be defined as non-persons and killed at the discretion and for the convenience of others.

It is essential that the constitutional protections attach from the moment of fertilization, by using that phrase or another of equal clarity. This is no mere academic point. Even the Supreme Court in *Roe v. Wade* admitted that if the unborn child is a person he cannot be killed by a legalized abortion in any case.[25] If the unborn child is not a person his life is no more protected by the Constitution than the life of a housefly. If constitutional protections attach to the unborn child, not at the moment of fertilization, but at some latter point, such as implantation in the womb, which generally occurs approximately seven days after fertilization, it will legitimize early abortions by pill, menstrual extraction, and other means. The intrauterine device, for instance, almost certainly operates by preventing implantation. It is, therefore, not a contraceptive but an abortifacient. With advancing technology, the abortion of the future is likely to be by pill rather than by surgery. If the constitutional protections do not attach at the earliest moment, that is, at fertilization, there will be no constitutional impediment to the licensing of abortion pills for use at early stages of pregnancy and if they are licensed for use at an early stage, they will be used at every stage. Clearly, therefore, constitutional protection must be restored unambiguously from the very beginning of life.

FIVE

Death and the Care of Defective Neonates

P.J. Riga

As THE TECHNOLOGICAL ABILITIES of modern medicine get more sophisticated, the problems of defective fetuses and neonates will become more troublesome.[1] While the idea that a woman may legally and morally abort her children if amniocentesis finds they may be defective enjoys widespread popularity among Americans, the logic of this mentality has already begun to spread to those children who are defective in some way and who still manage to be born.[2] But there are problems here as well. We have seen a case of the killing of one of a set of twins who was found to be defective, while the other was permitted to live;[3] on the other hand, fetal operations can correct many abnormalities thought previously to be unavoidable. This latter case poses acute problems for the abortion mentality since now the fetus is treated as independent patient and, to that extent, is considered a moral person. What of the technology that lowers the age of fetal viability from six months to five-and-a-half months; what becomes of our court decisions in these cases and of the notion of state interest?[4]

These are preliminary questions not directly in the purview of the pages which follow. We consider it imperative, however, that as a preface to these problems, we attempt to deal with a more foundational question of dying and death as it is viewed by modern medicine. This in turn will determine how medicine will tend to view the dying as well as born defective neonates. In fact, it will tell us much about the place of bioethics in the context of American culture.

In part two, we shall deal directly with the question of defective neonates as well as some suggested criteria to be used in establishing treatment or non-treatment for these children.

It should also be noted that these questions are hard questions of law and ethics and no clear and ready answers or solutions will be available to the doctors, other medical personnel, or ethics committees. What is imperative, however, is that we approach the question with a profound respect for *all* human life, the parents as well as the defective children. For if we are going to act like God, we should act like God with compassion, justice, and equality.

I

Each culture views death in a particular way because it views life in a particular way.[5] American culture is profoundly ambivalent about death, which is betrayed in the very language we use to describe death: we speak of "demise," "passing away," or say that someone is "no longer with us." In fact, our culture demands a "natural or timely death" as a basic right. It is seen as tragedy to die early, or in youth or in comparative youth (i.e., before the age of seventy). From a religious point of view, this statement is irrelevant; but our secular culture considers death an extreme social injustice which must be fought with every weapon at our disposal.[6]

In fact, the perceived function of medicine today—to help us ward off death—is part of the mythology of our culture born of secular humanism which either denies the reality of death or so clinically surrounds us with drugs and gadgetry that we and our families are no longer able—or willing—to participate in our own death or in the death of our loved ones. In fact, when medical technology fails, then the ominous thought of euthanasia ("easy or painless death") comes more and more into play in our culture. Since death has no communitarian rituals, nasia ("easy or painless death") comes utilitarianism is the order of the day at both ends of human existence.[7]

Our culture, precisely because it has lost its transcendent dimension in relation to death, has endowed medicine and doctors with quasi-religious goals and expectations which, by definition, they cannot meet or fulfill. For the first time in human history, health now means life in its struggle against death. The ideas that all sickness is potentially unto death, and that sickness unto death should be interfered with by the doctor, are both of recent origin, born of a culture which has lost its transcendent dimension to life and, therefore, to death as well. Stripped of transcendence, life is the ultimate value; death its ultimate and final tragedy.[8]

Traditionally, as long as Western culture was imbued with spiritual awareness, what people did to preserve their health or to cure their ills had little to do with what they did when they felt threatened by death. Medicine was ancillary to nature, helping to heal or helping men to die, because life and death were both accepted as an integral part of every human existence. The problem becomes infinitely more complex with the introduction of sophisticated modern technology which can keep people alive when they are no longer alive.[9] Since death is not seen as natural to the human condition, we have even greater difficulty in deciding when to remove these machines and begin caring for the dying. Since death is denied, care for the dying is not in the modern medical vocabulary.

The Renaissance stood the image of death and medicine on its head. Theocentrism was replaced by anthropocentrism which relied exclusively on humanism. Since God was relegated more and more to an unimportant fixture in the culture, the religious void is filled with enjoying life as much and as long as possible because life now is the supreme value. Doctors are no longer among the announcers of death, but are those who, for a price, will fight death to the very end. The ultimate product of all this is the technological clinic in which people die surrounded, not by family and the rites of the dying, but by medical wizardry which, while fighting death, denies its inevitable and imminent reality. The ever more expensive and intrusive medical technology deprives the individual and his family of the reality of his death; it is also an excuse for medical personnel not to be the messengers of the arrival of death, as they constantly monitor gauges and blips while neglecting the patient as a person who is dying and must die.[10]

Death is now seen in our culture as the ultimate evil because there is nothing beyond the present life. It must be fought with every industrial tool at our disposal; doctors are the soldiers or priests in this quasi-religious struggle against cancer, diabetes, heart disease, stroke, TB, cystic fibrosis, herpes—the list is endless. It is for this reason that doctors in our culture are the most esteemed and most handsomely paid professionals of all. With their new wizardry, they perform the exorcism of all forms of evil death; our major institutions constitute a gigantic defense program waged on behalf of humanity against unnatural death (i.e., before old age). We initiate crash programs to fight one disease after another, gearing up our medical technologies, and if all else fails against "evil death," then we can eliminate it by inflicted death at both ends of the life cycle: abortion and euthanasia. No one can even die without a doctor's permission in the form of a death certificate or autopsy. People must continously be on guard against evil death by constant checkups which makes them all perpetual patients of the doctors. We can now live and die only with the rituals of medical ministration: checkups, pap smears, breasts exams, rectal exams, X-rays, and so on. The analogy of medicine and religion is evident in all of this.

All of this is mostly patent nonsense precisely because medicine is endowed with quasi-religious goals—eternal life without pain or suffering—which by definition it cannot fulfill. Our culture uses the death image to impose a compulsory sociopolitical image of death. In fact, the production of natural death for all men has become the justification for social control: we must have doctor's certification to be born and to die; to go to school and to work; to emigrate and immigrate; to eat and to travel; to be married and to give birth. It has reached its apogee in the medical interventions of totally secularistic regimes such as the Soviet Union, where medicine is totally secular and political. The medical technologies are enlisted into the political process: anyone who objects or protests against the political regime is "sick," requiring the ministrations of psychiatric sciences.[11]

People are now deprived of their traditional vision of what constitutes health and death. Every attempt to make health delivery a personal and common experience is viewed with grave suspicion by the medical profession and the judiciary which has bought the modern view of medicine lock, stock, and barrel.

The modern doctor teaches the people about a pantheon of evils (clinical death), each one of which he will ban for a price. By his ministrations he urges people on in the search for the good life, a search which will be unending, and unfulfillable and will keep them his patients forever by constant checkups. Medicine has become the religious dogma around which the structuring rituals of our society are organized.

While death used to announce his coming by sickness unto death and each person's dignity demanded that he recognize the signs and prepare himself accordingly, institutional medicine now impresses on each person his duty to watch by constant checkups for any symptom that would require clinical defense. The dying man ceases to preside over the ceremonial of his own death, with family, friends, last rites, candles, loving forgiveness and pardon, but the doctor transforms it into the last stage of therapeutic pretensions. Deceived about the immiment, the patient dies surrounded not by loved ones and the rituals of the last sacraments, but by bleeps, drips, and warning buzzers.[12]

In many respects, this modern attitude toward death and dying greatly influences the way our culture approaches many of the problems of dying and death. If death is the ultimate evil with no sense of the sacred and transcendent, then euthanasia can be permitted at times, on the one hand, and on the other, an almost unreasonable desire not "to let go" and to use medical technology even when it makes no human sense to do so. In any case, the way a culture or society views dying and death will have no small influence on the way it decides to continue or terminate care on various categories of people: comatose patients, the conscious but pain-filled dying, and defective neonates.

Thus, death is a phenomenon more and more denied or escaped in the modern world. Just as a lie is an attempt to attach a patch on the vast cloth of reality, so too is modern medicine a form of denial of a basic and all-inclusive reality of human existence. Of course, only the appearance changes, not the reality, with fearsome consequences. Not only has modern medicine attempted to remove death from its basic place in its natural cycle of human existence; it has contributed thereby to the dismemberment and fragmentation of the traditional forms of community, especially kinship. It has removed more and more the communal properties of death, just as it has done for birth. Most Americans die not at home surrounded by the familiar and the beloved, but in hospitals, surrounded by the impersonal, the technological, and the futile. Even the sight of the dead—so important for grief and mourning so that the healing can begin—is more and more denied as we entrust everything to the professional mortician who seals the casket or cremates the remains which he instantly disperses so that there is not even a burial. We see notices like this one, for a person who has died of cancer: "Memorial services tomorrow at 3:00 p.m. No flowers please. Direct contributions to Win One Against Cancer Drive." Even the simple expressions of communal grief are denied and expunged.

This has its counterpoint in the modern preoccupation with health, health food, exercise, health clubs, spas, health jogging, biking clubs, tennis clubs, Weight Watchers, diet books— methods by the dozen—all of which is a manifestation of the unease with death. It is therefore not strange that on top of all book best-sellers for years now have been books and even records on dieting and weight loss, or exercise manuals (*Jane Fonda Exercise Book*). On the front cover of *Newsweek* (November 5, 1982) was the picture of an aging matron exercising her way to health. The story inside discussed clubs like these for old people who traditionally were the ones who, by their wisdom, were to prepare for death. Here was complete denial, even by the elderly, who are its most tragic victims.[13]

There is therefore nothing extraordinary in the fact that narcissism and egocentricity—which are much in evidence in all of these modern-day fads[14]—are the companions of the almost neurotic fear of death (which goes along with the modern fear of children, of marriage, of commitment, of life itself). Having abandoned the notion of death as a natural consequence of human life through these modern phenomena of denial, when death makes its inevitable appearance it is not as friend (St. Francis called it "Sister Death" because she was the opening to eternal life) but as the last enemy, to be fought with every measure, as ultimate tragedy and defeat, as humiliation and subjugation. It is no wonder that the reality of death must be denied at best and mortally feared at worst. The communal moorings of birth, marriage, and death which gave them their human meaning—above all *social* events, not *individual* or *physical* events—have long since disappeared. They have been replaced now with "methods" of childbirth, living together "arrangements," and the war on disease with its constant and perpetual checkup. This dread and fear of death comes from the isolation of the individual from communal moorings with their rituals which gave birth and death meaning. As Philippe Aries has shown, over the past ten centuries, dread, apprehension, and rejection of death have grown in almost precise relation to the growth of individualism and rejection of all forms of community (family, parish, neighborhood, locale).[15]

It should therefore be clear that there can be little hope of an acceptance of death in the modern Western world unless a sense of community has been restored in national, local, and kinship spheres. Until then, people will continue to live in a void—ego-gratifying, hedonistic, narcissistic, faddish—all the while utterly fearful of death, at once horrified and fascinated by this reality.

The sense and human meaning of death, like birth and marriage, comes from the communal ritual which surrounds these peak experiences of human existence. Modern life is utterly impersonal because it has destroyed the communal bases of the rituals of birth, marriage, and death. At death, they have been replaced with technology gadgetry and impersonal medical personnel checking tubes and fluids—everything but the real need of the patient. Physical birth is only the first stage of acknowledgment in the Christian community, which recognizes its own only by a ritual of rebirth in baptism which is the child's acceptance into the rights and duties of the Christian community. In modern culture, concentration on methods of childbirth has replaced an emphasis on its meaning in the life of the community because there is no community. Nuclear, separatist marriage—when there is one at all—is no longer celebrated in the community of the church and in the presence of kin and clan who by these rites introduce the couple into the large community of ethics, ecclesia, and neighborhood. People live alone, away from blood relatives, in huge and impersonal apartments or condo complexes; their religious faith or practice has utterly atrophied or is artificial because it is no longer nurtured at communal roots. Today over twenty percent of adult Americans live alone and the numbers grow as isolation increases. Adult communities which exclude children are epidemic; up to two-thirds of rental units in America simply exclude children. How can there by any sense of tradition and community in normal circumstances without the presence of children?

Such isolation is the death of all forms of community: familial, ecclesial, regional, and local. With the death of community and the isolation of Americans, the inevitable fear of death grows; it no longer has human meaning, since birth, marriage, and death are essentially social and individual events.[16]

It is in the light of this reality of denial and isolation that one must begin to understand the problems of the new technology and bioethics. When there no longer is a sense of transcendence and the sacred surrounding human life, then the problems of death and dying, of the comatose and the retarded, and of defective unborn and newborn children become more difficult to resolve and deal with. After all, the "sanctity" of human life is just that: it is something greater than life itself. It was originally a religious phrase: all human life is somehow related to God and must be utterly respected by man. With this religous sense long since absent, these questions become much more problematic.

II

For the first time, along with the case of *Infant Doe* in Indiana, a case of Siamese twins who were allegedly denied food and oxygen at their parents' request has now come to the attention of the courts. The deformed Siamese twins were born May 5, 1981, to a Danville, Illinois, physician and his wife; the twins were found to be neglected children by a judge on June 5, 1981, but, curiously, the same judge found no neglect on the part of the parents who knew or should have known what was happening to their children in the hospital. Someone was responsible for withholding ordinary food and drink. Presumably at this point in the neglect proceedings we do not know who.

The State took temporary custody of the sons of Dr. Robert Mueller and his wife, Pamela Schopp, when a social worker acting on an anonymous call visited Lakeview Medical Center and found evidence of neglect.[17] In fact, what she found was that the Siamese twins were denied food and drink to the point where their ribs were protruding. In effect, they were being allowed to starve.

The Siamese twins were joined at the waist and shared three legs. More ominously for their future, they shared a common digestive system and some vital organs.[18] While custody was being decided, the children were examined and cared for at Children's Memorial Hospital in Chicago to determine whether they could be separated. Medical experts gave a negative prognosis for separation. In fact, the final resolution of the case indicated that no one was responsible for the neglect: the parents were finally awarded custody of the twins and allowed to take them home.

The ethical and legal issues here are momentous since there are no recorded cases in which either parents or physicians have been held liable for failure to maintain children who have been born with defects or conditions such that the parents are unwilling to live with them. In a sense, what we have here is the other side of the coin of the Philip Becker[19] case where a young Down's syndrome 12-year-old boy was refused corrective heart surgery by the parents. Their action was upheld by the California Trial Court on the precedent of the *Saikewicz* case for no other reason than that the boy was retarded. The difference is that in the *Mueller* case, the defect was detected immediately and the attempted remedy was a sort of postnatal abortion. This practice is not new, as we shall see in a moment. Involuntary euthanasia on defective neonates has been going on for well over a decade at various university clinics and hospitals. It is only now that it has been brought to the notice of public authorities and some legal and moral standards must be set up for treating or not treating such children.

The case of *Infant Doe* from Bloomington, Indiana, was factually similar.[20] A retarded Down's syndrome child was allowed to die by denying it the elemental human demands of food and drink. It was originally the decision of his or her parents which the appellate Court of Indiana refused to stay or prevent. The child died of dehydration and starvation before the U.S. Supreme Court could intervene. The legal question is not "moot" but is precedent in Indiana.

The facts of the case clearly show that *Infant Doe* was not dying at all. If the child was dying and beyond the scope of our healing process, then there would have been no legal or moral problem at all. As with all the dying, we would then withdraw the useless technology of medicine, make the patient as comfortable as possible, and let nature take its course. The lawyer for the parents at first claimed that the child had only a "50-50 chance of survival" with a simple operation to repair an esophogeal fistula. In fact, this figure was incorrect. Infant Doe could have surgery with an excellent chance of success, according to expert medical testimony. In sum, Infant Doe was allowed to dehydrate and starve to death because he or she was retarded. Thus the parents and their doctors decided to "let nature take its course." This was in reality a twist in the evident meaning of the English language. If one withdraws food and drink from any child, it will die and the cause will be the refusal, not "nature." As little information as possible was given by all concerned: lawyers, parents, hospital personnel, and authorities. The reason was clear: for the first time in the history of the United States, an appellate court had ratified out and out euthanasia for the sole reason that the subject was retarded. Since Infant Doe died of dehydration and starvation, the withholding of food and drink was the direct cause of death. To add to the tragedy of the case, we have the perversion of language: a lawyer, counsel for the parents, called all this "a case of love."

In October, 1973, there appeared an article entitled "Moral and Ethical Dilemmas in the Special Care Nursery."[21] The authors reported that some 43 (14 percent) of the 249 consecutive infant deaths at the Yale University School of Medicine Special Care Nursery were deaths related to withholding treatment. The parents and physicians in a joint decision decided that the infant's prognosis for "meaningful life" was very poor and therefore treatment was to be rejected. There are, however, very few legal cases where such an argument has been made.

In one case, *Maine Medical Center v. Houle*,[22] a male infant was born without a left eye or a left ear, with a deformed left hand and a tracheoesophageal fistula. Without surgical repair (a minor operation), the infant would die. The parents were informed and they directed the physician not to operate on the child and to withhold feedings and intravenous fluids. The Center petitioned the State Superior Court for a temporary restraining order to maintain intravenous feedings pending the Court's ruling on the question of surgical intervention. The child developed seizures which were interpreted as brain damage. The Court granted the restraining order and ordered the parents that they not interfere with the efforts of the physicians to perform surgery and that to do so would constitute child neglect. The pediatrician notified the Court of the severity of the prognosis and the condition of the child. The judge ruled that "the issue is not the prospective quality of life to be preserved." *Houle* held that the *evaluation* (i.e., the value to be assigned to this life or any life) is beyond the physician's scope because "quality of life" judgments are beyond the physician's medical expertise, and that withholding consent to the operation would constitute "neglect" on the part of the parents. In the words of the Court: "The most basic right enjoyed by every human being is the right to life itself." The Court acted as *parens patriae* and appointed a guardian to consent to surgery and enjoin the parents from interfering with any future medical treatment. The infant died on February 24, 1974. In *Mueller, Infant Doe, Houle,* and *Becker,* the parents were particularly angered over interference in "a strictly private and familial matter." In regard to these cases, some remarks should be made.

First of all, we are here no longer in a *Roe* situation since all of these children in *Mueller* and other cases have been born and, presumably, have met the constitutional requirement for personhood with full rights, including a right to life. Leaving the fate of such persons to the interested discretion of parents and doctors is a complete and arbitrary denial of due process and equal protection. What is at work here is a quality of life argument as decided by the interested parties, parents and doctors, for which there is little legal precedent. We are not dealing here with a "prolongation of dying" of terminally ill patients, but with children presumed to have a diminished human capacity.

Secondly, any legal response to this question of involuntary euthanasia depends on our expectations of what law can and should accomplish in this situation.[23] In the final analysis such broad determination of law as public policy should be made by a legislature or by the people themselves. Are these defective children a definable class? Are certain instances of withholding treatment morally justified or socially desirable, and who is to make this decision fairly and impartially after a consideration of all the facts? Legal rules must focus on criteria, procedures, and decision-making processes for implementing a *social* policy of this kind of involuntary passive euthanasia. These politico-moral questions must be answered before we can being to think about a legal policy or a juridical final determination.

Courts are ill-equipped to consider and determine these basic questions of social desirability and public policy since they do not have the scope of information and input necessary for such decisions. These are hard questions of social policy which must be faced by the legislature. Failure to do so only makes the work of courts necessary but confusing, as the case law in similar areas has been clearly shown. Failure by the legislature to establish public policy in this area also contributes to lack of objective standards to be followed by parents, hospitals, and medical personnel. Yet when dealing with defective neonates it is truly difficult to give general rules and standards. Standards in general there must be, but more important still are the values and intent of the decision-makers, since so many of these cases are on the borderline where general rules are inapplicable.

It should also be clear that the right to privacy simply cannot be asserted by this whole group of parents when the right of some other citizens (their children) are being undermined and destroyed without due process. Thus, some presumptions and objective criteria must be set up to insure a fair and impartial hearing, where, since the subjects of rights (children) can give no consent to their own treatment, a substituted consent of some form can be found. I shall try to outline these standards in the final section of this paper.

Substituted consent for these defective neonates is really a misnomer. There is no possibility of finding out what they would want, were they able to see and understand their present condition. Nor are we here in the area of prolongation of death where the medical prognosis for recovery or a return to cognitive and sapient life as in *Quinlan* is reasonably excluded. We are dealing here with persons who will lead, at best, diminished lives as in the *Saikewicz* case, but for whom treatment will prolong their lives. Therefore, it is crucial to understand that any election not to treat defective neonates outside of the "poor medical prognosis" context is really based on a "quality of life" determination which is essentially a question of social and, therefore, legislative policy. It is also a question of value choice and the meaning of death and life which was discussed in section one above.

It may well be that as a society we will decide not to treat certain classes of persons (e.g., severely retarded or senile), but the legislative guidelines and standards should be reasonably well-defined and the circumstances clear where treatment will not be refused except in the most hopeless medical cases. It may also well be that our society is acutely afraid to articulate such guidelines for a variety of reasons and is therefore willing to consign these cases either to the private discretion of some (parents and doctors) or to the courts. The difficulty with this is that in the former, neonates are given no fundamental due process which will fairly safeguard their right to life; while the latter solution has led to judicial confusion concerning the standards to be applied in similar cases.[24]

In cases of defective newborns, some courts might seek to ask, as the *Quinlan* court did, what the newborn would decide (substitute consent) were he capable of doing so.[25] We might want to ask why a defective infant might want to die. First of all, this is already a false question because, aside from the fanciful nature of the answer, we are in grave danger of projecting our own values onto the child who has absolutely no basis for the fears and horrors we might have for ourselves in a similar state. This implication of the quality of life argument presupposes, first, a basic higher level of health, consciousness, awareness, and so on, and then a degeneration from this state. By definition, this state is absent from the defective newborn who might well be happy and satisfied to live out his limited human potential, having never realized what he is missing. This can only be realized by those who have in fact realized the higher levels of intelligence and human consciousness and who now project *their* potential lack or loss on those who never had it in the first place. We are in grave danger of confusing *our* suffering (physician, parents, judge, general public) with that of the child who has never known any other existence and, for all we know, would be perfectly content to live as he is. In fact, it is well-known that many of these children are capable of giving and receiving love and generally taking care of themselves. In protected or sheltered environments, many of them even lead productive lives. But all this becomes a basic question in classical public policy of how far as a society do we wish to revere, treat, and protect such people.[26]

It is also true that there are correlations between parental acceptance of their handicapped children and such factors as religion, social class, and the presence of supportive friends and relatives. As one expert put it: "But parents learn to value and love their children as they live with them."[27] In any case, there is no clear or convincing reason why a diminished future should bother the person who has known no other level of life. No convincing arguments for their way of dealing with the problem have been advanced by those who want to kill such persons "for their own good" or, what amounts to the same thing, not to treat them as they would other "normal" children or adults similarly situated and thus "allow them to die." More to the point, as a society we should be terribly skeptical about a strong group (parents and doctors) who want to kill, not treat, or do away with a weaker group (defective newborns) "for their own good." History is too replete with atrocious examples to take this argument very seriously either as a matter of law or public policy. In the words of P. Foot:

With children who are born with Down's Syndrome it is, however, quite different [than children soon to die]. Most of these are able to live on for quite awhile in a reasonably contented way, remaining like children all of their lives, but capable of affectionate relationships and able to play games all of their lives, but capable of affectionate relationships and able to play games and perform simple tasks. The fact is, of course, that the doctors who recommend against lifesaving procedures for handicapped infants are usually thinking not of them but rather of their parents, and of other children in the family, or of the "burden on society" if the children survive. So it is not for their sake but to avoid trouble to others that they are allowed to die.[28]

The easiest cases to decide in this area are those children whose "medical prognosis is wretchedly bad," and who would die in a very short time no matter what we would do (e.g., acephalic newborns). When this basic medical decision or prognosis is made in good faith and according to accepted medical standards, all support systems (outside of those necessary for the comfort of the child) may be legally and morally discontinued since medical procedures no longer have any human meaning or significance. One is not obligated to do the futile or to continue the useless. This was the basic conclusion of the *Quinlan* court as it set up the procedure to be followed in such cases without further judicial intervention and can be applied to this situation as well.[29]

But there are the much more difficult cases of the mentally or physically defective who will live diminished lives but from whom accepted and comparatively simple procedures are withheld so that they are "allowed to die," when those procedures could have prolonged their admittedly limited lives. This seems to have been the situation in the *Mueller* and *Infant Doe* cases.

The problem to be faced in these tragic situations is moral and legal at the same time. The moral question is what category of patients do we—as a society—simply not wish to treat? Perhaps we cannot face this question directly so we leave it to courts, much like the Americans of the nineteenth century left the moral question of whether slaves were human beings to the

Supreme Court. The answer these Americans got was *Dred Scott*. The answer we are beginning to receive in the case of defective neonates is that since their quality of life is so bad they should be allowed to die. We are beginning to see a subtle erosion away from the presumption for these children to one against these children. Moral questions simply cannot be shirked by a society and these categories of human beings (the senile aged, the severely mentally and physically handicapped neonates) will simply not go away. Given our sophisticated technology, their number will in fact increase.

Secondly, there is an important legal question here as well. What is happening in the courts in the few cases handed down concerning defective persons is 1) they are not being treated the same as other "normal" people in the same situation (*Becker, Mueller, Saikewicz, Infant Doe*) and 2) the standard used in these cases is subjective and dangerous ("quality of life") for the groups themselves. It is the courts themselves who are therefore creating great equal protection difficulties in the way they are treating these people.

What should be clear, at once, is that parents and their physicians alone cannot be trusted to make such decisions for another human being. Both of these groups have a significant conflict of interest which impairs their judgment negatively in a life and death situation such as in the *Mueller* case where decisions affecting the children must be made comparatively soon after birth. The parents' interest may well be to save their own psychological and economic life as well as that, perhaps, of their other children, past and future. It may well be that in that sense such children become a "burden." But the question to be asked is: to whom? This does not make parents evil but simply bad decision-makers under the circumstances. Similarly, the physician is usually too much affected by those whose feelings are most visible and tangible—the parents—to be a very objective articulator of the child's interest. In fact, various studies show that most physicians tend not to want to treat such infants since they represent a failure for the physicians. At least they consider such infants better off dead, even though some parents in fact do *not* share such views of their physicians without, however, ever saying so.[30] If these studies are correct, we have a significant problem when many treating physicians, without the guidance of some objective standards, believe in the loose thinking of the "quality of life" theory. The threat to these neonates in such a situation is obvious.

Who then can be trusted with such decisions? The *Quinlan* decision at least provided this protection for incompetents who are in a prolongation of dying situation by a diffusion of decision-making representing a societal consensus; by analogy, the same reasoning may be applied to newborn defective children who are in the same situation. While acknowledging the parents as appropriate guardians and protecting their right to *participate* in deciding to end treatment which is medically useless, the court stated that such a decision would be legally valid only if it had the approval of a hospital ethics committee. Whatever one thinks of the final function of such a committee, it does recognize that one physician and family cannot make such important decisions alone with no protection to the helpless child.[31] In other words, this method of decision diffusion is not to be construed as an unwillingness to assume personal responsibility on the part of parents and physicians, but rather as an incipient effort to reach some form of societal consensus on these edges of life issues and to take them out of the *exclusive* hands of those (parents, physicians) who have a vested negative interest in the case. This would fit in well with Professor Robertson's suggestion that for the most extreme cases, society through the legislature or courts should recognize certain objective criteria where treatment can be refused:

> But, just as authoritative and specific criteria have eased the physician's determination of when brain death has occurred, the risks of delegating treatment to parents, physicians, or committees can be similarly lessened if specific criteria are developed to describe defective characteristics in the familial or institutional situations in which treatment may be withheld from defective infants.

Perhaps this is as far as we can go. Perhaps to acknowledge openly that we are willing to treat the retarded or the senile or severely defective neonates differently from the "normal" patient is so offensive to society's view of the equality of citizens that its explicit acknowledgment is impossible. We then need to rationalize a way to treat them differently, and the notion of substituted judgment seems to be one such means invented by the courts. If we can establish some minimal standards, perhaps this would be as far as we can go with rules.

Moreover, it would also seem part of the legal obligation for any informed consent by the parents that they be objectively and fully informed of the possibility of taking many of the defective newborns home and having, at least in some cases, a wholesome family experience. Recent studies have show this to be much more prevalent than previously suspected either by physicians or by the general public. As another expert has put it:

Those who have lived with the handicapped seem to reject any necessary incompatibility between being handicapped and leading a worthwhile life, a conclusion that ought to be taken into account by those charged with making decisions about "the right of life" of infants with birth defects.[32]

There should at least be one *caveat* in this whole discussion of newborn defective children, and that is how society has come to view the handicapped—or will view them in the not so distant future. It is evident that better medical care, surgery, disease control, and technology have enabled many more of the handicapped to live than ever before. On the other hand, there must be an acceptance of defective children in society as well. It is the classical example of the threat to certain categories of human beings from the strong against the weak. For instance, the mongoloid or Down's syndrome child, the most stigmatized of the retarded, physically and socially, represents an assault to middle-class strivings and aspirations and to culturally determined goals. He is seen as an impediment to social mobility.

Zuk's studies[33] of attitudes of Protestant and Catholic mothers of retarded children showed the latter to be far more accepting of their children than the former. He concluded that Catholics were more accepting "due to the explicit absolution from personal guilt offered by their religious belief" and because a Catholic mother could accept the child in a framework of "a test of her religious faith . . . a special gift of God."[34] Moreover, women are much more accepting of defective children than men—no matter at what cultural or intellectual level.[35]

But much also depends on cultural factors as well:

> Parents, especially in the middle class, expect more intimacy and perfection in their children. The appearance of a defective newborn is more self-devastating than in an earlier time when a family needed more children and when children were not so regarded as expressions of the selves of parents.[36]

Thus middle-class culture stresses the "perfect" and the "normal" and loathes more than ever before the imperfect and the defective. With the perfection of the technique of amniocentesis, newborn defectives are more and more looked upon as "mistakes" that could have been prevented by selective abortion, which is accepted by the vast majority of the American people. It is reasonable to conclude that attitudes toward defective newborns will become progressively more negative as the processes of prenatal diagnosis improves and those who are not "perfect" are aborted. The failure and guilt already associated with this situation will only grow now that all this could have been easily detected and "eliminated." One can therefore expect an increase in the number of parents who will attempt to instruct physicians not to treat—even minimally—a seriously defective child. As one expert has put it: "Most parents in our society if given the choice would prefer abortion of an affected fetus to a sick child who requires any but the most trivial treatment." The preference is likely to become more definite with rapidly changing attitudes to abortion at a time when the low risks of amniocentesis will become fully established and when simple abortion techniques become available.

Since the abortion of the defective fetus is so widely accepted in our society, morally and legally, we are now also becoming accustomed to withdrawing medical care from these defective children who still manage to be born. Speaking of nontreatment and even the active euthanasia of defective newborns, one expert has commented:

> The question remains, then, whether the introduction of euthanasia for spina bifida children, in strictly controlled circumstances, would lead to the wide use of euthanasia in other circumstances, simply as a result of a change in moral attitudes? The comparison with abortion makes this difficult to deny. . . . It is noteworthy that the attitude of a very considerable section of the medical profession toward abortion has almost totally reversed itself in the space of only a few years. The acceptance of abortion in the profession today seems almost unconceivable when viewed from the standpoint of a quarter of a century ago. It is perfectly conceivable that the profession's declared attitude to euthanasia will equally reverse itself.[37]

This mentality also threatens the future emphasis on cure and grappling with the problem, to an emphasis on prevention, detection, and abortion to rid us of the problem radically. This subtle shift looks harmless enough until this mentality confronts what it has not been able, as yet, to detect: defective neonates.

This theory is indeed a powerful wedge: once the law recognizes the right to actively end the human life of the defective unborn, the logic of such a utilitarian ethic will be difficult, if not impossible, to control with regard to the defective who are, in fact, born. This has created acceptance, if not sympathy, for those who abort the possibly defective unborn; this attitude cannot help but spill over into attitudes affecting those defective children who happen to have been born. Perhaps the best suggestion, once again, comes from Professor Robertson:

> If recognized by the courts or legislatures, such criteria [to describe defective characteristics] would represent a collective social judgment, rather than idiosyncratic choices of parents and committees, as to when social costs outweigh individual benefits. To achieve legislative consensus, the criteria for death should necessarily be narrow, reaching only the extreme cases. Further protection can be obtained by a procedure that insures that the required clinical findings are accurately assessed, for example, by certification of two non-attending physicians before treatment is withheld.[38]

The real problem is to restrict this measure severely by law to the extreme cases, which many thoughtful physicians believe do exist.

The AMA Judicial Council has tried to deal with the most extreme of these cases: "A decision whether to treat a severely defective infant and exert maximal efforts to sustain life" should be left to the parents. No one could quarrel with this, as long as they are fully informed of all possibilities, and the decision is restricted to a very narrow category of cases. But this is not what is beginning to happen in this field. Outside of "maximal care," we have rather simple medical procedures being eliminated in order to bring about death; and, as in the *Mueller* and *Infant Doe* cases, the withholding of ordinary food and drink. It is these latter hard cases which cause all the legal and moral problems. We need some clear procedures in this painful area.

Such legal procedures will help minimize the risks to others, but, still, the real danger here is the outgrowth of measures already morally and legally accepted in our society against defective human life which is unborn; it seems only a small but logical step to correct what we missed only a few hours before. In the final analysis, this is not a direct problem of law, but of society's attitude toward defective human life, which then comes to affect the law. Once we start down the road, for whatever reason, it is difficult to control its logical application to those who have managed to be born with defects.

III

Even after the few cases relating to defective neonates are carefully examined, there emerge few clear and sure guidelines for physicians and parents to follow in knowing when to treat or not to treat. The following guidelines are legal and moral, garnered from some of the cases, as well as from good medical practice.[39]

(1) As a general rule, parents are in fact and in law the principal decision-makers for the health and care of their children. This principle is well established, whether in natural or in constitutional law. Outside of the exceptions given below, their desires and wishes are to be followed as the general rule.

(2) The physician has a legal and moral responsibility to be open and truthful to the parents of defective neonates. This calls for full disclosure and informed consent on the part of parents—and this at the earliest possible time after the preliminary diagnosis has been established. All future medical options should be outlined for the parents or guardian, including nontreatment, and the risks, benefits, chances of success, and consequences of each medical procedure available. The objective of this is to give parents the fullest information and possible options available to them so that they can fully and knowingly consent to treatment or nontreatment.

(3) While it is difficult to determine always what "accepted medical standards" are at any one time (what is extraordinary today may be ordinary procedure tomorrow), the presumption is that the physician is acquainted with the ordinary standard of the profession. If nontreatment or treatment is within that range, the doctor may comply with the parents' wishes. If the doctor is uncertain as to prognosis, he should consult another, independent doctor, who is to perform an independent examination of the child (by "independent" is meant disinterested in

the outcome, whether for research, transplantation, or for any other reason). It would also be of great value in any area of doubt for the doctor to have an ethics committee whom he could consult, both for decision diffusion, dispassion, and some expert input in this delicate matter. Such a committee could be composed of a cross section of legal, medical, ethical, and religious talent.

(4) If the parents decide not to treat and to permit the child to die, it is imperative that the doctor seek the independent evaluation of another disinterested doctor before he acquiesces in the desire of the parents (presuming, of course, that the course of action is supported by good and accepted medical standards).

(5) If the doctor and the independent examining doctor conclude that nontreatment by the doctor is not in conformity with accepted medical procedure, then the attending doctor must point this situation out to the parents and explain the reasons why this is so. If the parents insist nonetheless on nontreatment, the doctor or hospital administrator should not hesitate to petition a court of competent jurisdiction for the appointment of a guardian to consent to treatment.

(6) What are the standards to be used to withhold treatment? This is difficult, because these standards are always evolving. Indeed, it is in the very nature of medical progress that they do evolve for the better. But lacking any absolute, legal standards, the following may be safely followed:

—Where death will come about imminently, no matter what we do, there is no legal or moral obligation to treat or to continue to treat, outside of basic procedures to make the child comfortable.

—Where there is no medical possibility or probability—given our present knowledge of medicine—of the child ever achieving any cognitive or sapient stage of conscious realization, no treatment need be given, nor need treatment be continued. Once again, we are held to what is humanly possible, not to what can or will happen sometime and somewhere down the historical road.

—Many eminent authorities argue that where the child has no reasonable possibility of ever being able to participate to *any* degree in human relationships with others, no treatment need be commenced nor treatment continued, beyond basic comfort of the child.

—Where there is no medical possibility or probability of alleviating what reasonable medical judgment would consider to be an intolerable level of continued suffering, the same judgment should obtain as in the above cases. Human intervention must be for good (*primum non nocere*), and if there is little probability that good will come about, then it is both futile and cruel to act further on this human being.

However, in this last condition, precisely because there is a dimension of the subjective involved, another independent doctor should examine the case along with, if possible, the hospital ethics committee, if it exists. This condition should also be seen in the light of good and accepted medical standards.

(7) To alleviate the intolerable decision-making in so charged and painfilled an atmosphere, parents should be told that the question of long-term custody of the child can be settled later. This would allow parents to consent to care at a crucial juncture, rather than forcing them to participate in the child's death as the price of not assuming long-term custody. By emphasizing that the appropriateness of custody must be assessed continuously throughout the child's life, the parents could more comfortably commit themselves to the child, one day at a time, without feeling boxed into the situation.

(8) If the doctor concludes that treatment will be ineffective, but the parents insist that it be undertaken, the doctor should acquiesce to these desires, as long as the treatment does no further harm nor causes further suffering to the child. If it does, he should, in conscience, refuse to perform, and speak to the parents about obtaining a new doctor.

(9) Under no circumstances should an active agent, or otherwise lethal procedure, whose direct object is to either kill or help terminate the life of the child, be administered. Much here depends on the *intent* of the doctor and medical personnel,

which no court of law can really control or regulate. For instance, it is certainly legally and morally permissible to administer a large quantity of pain-killing drug, if the direct intent of the doctor is to in fact alleviate pain, even though it has, as an indirect effect, the shortening of the life of the patient.

(10) In all cases basic comfort and care should be given. This should include food and water in all but the cases where it is actually painful for the child to receive even these. This should include warmth, physical affection, and sanitation.

(11) Above all, the major rule in this area is that treatment is to be withheld only in the clearest and most compelling cases of hopelessness, using the above-mentioned safeguarding criteria. If there is *any* doubt in all of this, it should be resolved in favor of the child, for his life, and for his best interests.

SIX

"Why Will Ye Die, O House of Israel?" Euthanasia in the Eighties

Harold O.J. Brown

R UNNING THROUGH THE BIBLE, both the Old and the New Testaments, are two themes that sometimes appear to be in conflict with one another. Both individually and taken together they are in conflict with the direction of modern society. One of them is individual responsibility; the other is corporate solidarity. "Fathers shall not be put to death for their sons, nor shall sons be put to death for their fathers; everyone shall be put to death for his own sin." Thus we read in the Law of Moses, Deuteronomy 24:16. But in the same Law, indeed, in the Ten Commandments themselves, God warns his people, "I, the Lord your God, am a jealous God, visiting the iniquity of the fathers on the children, and on the third and fourth generations of those who hate me" (Dt 5:9).

Death is an individual matter. As the Negro spiritual puts it, "You got to meet it all alone." But there is also something collective about it. A century ago, Arthur Conan Doyle, himself a physician, put these words in the mouth of Sherlock Holmes's friend Dr. Watson: death is "that dark alley where all paths meet. . . ." John Donne wrote, "Every man's death diminishes me." For Donne, the Negro spiritual, and Dr. Watson, death was both deeply personal and individual, and yet the common lot that somehow relates us all to one another.

The twentieth century is—or is supposed to be—an age of individuality. In the Me Generation, slogans vary in grace from the simple but direct advocacy of "doing your own thing" to the more sophisticated praise of concepts such as self-fulfillment. Unfortunately for our age and its illusions, the individuality we seek and proclaim in one area is rapidly being eaten away in other and more final ways. "You arrive," wrote Rainer Maria Rilke, "you find a life, ready-made, all you have to do is to put it on." And at the end of life, individuality truly becomes illusory. "You want to go, or are forced to do so; now, no straining: Voilá votre mort, monsieur. We die, just as it comes. We die the death that belongs to the disease. . . . Naturally, just like in a factory. With such a gigantic production, the individual death is not so well finished, but that's not the point. The volume is what counts."

On taking his departure from the Hebrew people that he had led out of Egypt, as they were about to cross the literal River Jordan into the earthly Promised Land, Moses sood on the bank of his own personal, private, metaphorical Jordan, "chilly and cold," which "chills the body, but not the soul." His charge to his people was this: "Choose life, in order that you may live, you and your descendants" (Dt 30:19).

Choose life: it seems a natural enough thing. How could anyone do otherwise? But people do otherwise. Repeatedly the prophets reproached the people, puzzled as well as indignant: "Why will ye die, O house of Israel?" (Ez 18:31).

Individual responsibility and corporate solidarity: concepts that are not easy to harmonize with one another, and neither of which is congenial to our society. It is rather as the captured British aviator said to the Italian officer in *The Best of Enemies*: "No one likes war, but you people don't even make the effort!" No one likes personal responsibility, especially when individual decisions have implications for all the rest of society, or of humanity. In our day, most people aren't even making the effort. And nowhere is this failure more evident than in the steps our society is taking in the direction of euthanasia.

Euthanasia:
A Brief History of the Idea

In the wake of the Tylenol poisonings in Illinois, the radio carried the voice of Surgeon General C. Everett Koop, warning the general public to exercise great caution with respect to "pharmaceuticals that you intend to ingest." The precautions recommended by Dr. Koop were admirable. But one does wonder how many of the unfortunate victims, before being poisoned, would have recognized that they were forming the intention to ingest a pharmaceutical. We are familiar with the fact that the pro-abortion movement finds it much easier to market the disposability of a fetus than a baby, and more recently, the less sensitive euphemism "products of conception" has been introduced. Before society forms the intent to ingest "euthanasia," it should make sure what kind of a pharmaceutical this is.

The term *eu-thanasia*, from the Greek prefix *eu-*, indicating good, and *thanatos*, death, was coined to stand for the practice or institution of the good death. In a way, the very concept is antithetical to biblical religion, for the Bible presents death as the penalty for sin and describes it as "the last enemy" (1 Cor 15:26). Nevertheless, both classical philosophers and early Christians had the idea of the "good" death. It was, however, never thought that death itself was good. When Odysseus met Achilles in Hades and congratulated him on his eminent position among the shades, the hero replied, "Better to be the servant of a mean man in life than the lord among all these dead gone." The pagan philosophers emphasized the value of dying honorably and courageously, but death was not good.

The Christian idea of a happy death is unobjectionable. Francis Bacon called this "spiritual euthanasia," thus using what we now see as a bad word—meaning killing, or specifically mercy killing—to cover a good idea—spiritual comfort for the dying. Bacon also spoke of "natural euthanasia," by which he meant the help of the physician and others to allow the *moriturus,* the one about to die, to die as comfortably and as tranquilly as possible.

Both "natural euthanasia" and "spiritual euthanasia," in Bacon's language, are not merely morally unobjectionable, but highly desirable. Soon, however, we shall encounter procedures, also called euthanasia, that are questionable, objectionable, unethical, immoral, illegal—and evil. Thus we are going to have to learn (a) to distinguish between varieties of euthanasia, and (b) to recognize that the distinction popularized today—that between "passive" and "active" euthanasia—is *not* the crucial distinction.

Degrees of Euthanasia

At this point, permit me to introduce some terminology of my own. You may not have heard it yet, but if you haven't, you may find it helpful. We shall speak of first-, second-, and third-degree euthanasia.

First-degree euthanasia embraces what Bacon called "natural" and "spiritual" euthanasia. It is never culpable. It involves no "medical" or therapeutic measures that might in any way hasten the death of a *moriturus.* Third-degree euthanasia involves "medical"—or pharmacological, if we may use a less benign term—measure intended to bring about death—usually swiftly and painlessly—in one who is not a *moriturus,* who is not about to die. It is killing, it is morally culpable, and—at the moment—it is criminal.

Second-degree euthanasia and third-degree euthanasia differ from first-degree euthanasia in that they both involve medical measures. First and second degree euthanasia differ from third degree in that they both involve dying persons, *morituri,* while third degree does not.

It is thus second-degree euthanasia that involves both

morituri, those who are about to die, and medical measures, taken or not taken. It is within second-degree euthanasia that the most difficult moral and legal problems arise. It is necessary to make careful distinctions. The most common distinction— and a very misleading one—is that between measures taken and measures not taken. Where medical measures are not taken, or are discontinued—which can be, and often is, medically, morally, and legally proper—this is called "passive euthanasia." When measures are taken, and speedier death results, this is called "active euthanasia"—it is usually medically, morally, and legally culpable. This common distinction between passive euthanasia, deemed proper, and active euthanasia, deemed improper, is misleading and should be avoided. It is misleading because it confuses some issues and fails to distinguish others.

Confusion: the passive-active terminology confuses the question of means; it appears to make the morality of euthanasia hinge on whether it involves *means,* i.e., therapy. Without means, passive euthanasia is all right. "Passive euthanasia"—a term to which I object—is all right, but not because it involves no means. Also, passive euthanasia is not really mercy killing, but only euthanasia as Bacon's natural and spiritual euthanasia is euthanasia.

Distinction: the passive-active terminology is misleading because it fails to distinguish what is so important, namely, the *intent* of the medical care personnel. Intent is crucial, and it is hard to determine intent.

A Preliminary Comparison Between Abortion and Euthanasia

As the great but little-known jurist, P. Clodius Pulcher, wrote in *De Legibus Romanorum,* "Casus durus legem malam facit"—a hard case makes a bad law. (You may pardon me for inventing P. Clodius Pulcher—I wanted to add classical emphasis to that very important legal maxim, hard cases make bad law—the curse of the Supreme Court, inasmuch as only hard cases are sent up, many bad laws must inevitably come down.)

Nowhere is the truth of Pulcher's principle more evidently demonstrated than in abortion law—or, more specifically, in the arguments of the pro-abortionists. Almost invariably, very hard cases are cited to justify bad laws. In fact, the vast majority of abortions are not hard cases—at most, they are convenience cases. In euthanasia, however, *omnis casus durus*—every case is hard. Therefore, it is crucial, before we are plunged into the midst of a hard case, to consider some of the principles that must be recognized if we are not to end up with very bad laws indeed.

To repeat our comments on degrees (like burns, not like murder) in second-degree euthanasia, what is important is not methodology—not whether a specific treatment is withheld or provided, but the *intent* of the attending health care personnel. We all understand that comforting the dying, at one end of the terminal care spectrum, is not merely totally unobjectionable, but is a moral imperative. And—for the present—we still understand that the killing of those who are not dying, but who have been found to be "useless eaters," not possessing a satisfactory "quality of life"—something we shall shortly define as "third-degree euthanasia"—is totally unacceptable. The difficulty lies in the fact that the distinction between "passive" and "active" euthanasia is a false distinction and will permit us to slide imperceptibly across the barrier that divides mere acquiescence in the inevitability of death from deliberate inducing of death in those who are not dying. There is an important distinction within the bounds of what we are calling second-degree euthanasia, and it is by observing this distinction that we may be able to stop our drift from the first-degree to the third. But it is not a distinction between different kinds of treatment, or between treatment and nontreatment, but a distinction in intent, within the minds of the health care personnel and other directly concerned persons. Because it is a distinction in intent, it is hard to grapple with, and very difficult to regulate or control by law; because it is a distinction of vital—or we could say, mortal—importance, it is absolutely necessary that we find a way of dealing with it.

Stages or Varieties of Second-Degree Euthanasia

To repeat, first-degree and second-degree euthanasia have in common that both deal with patients who are in the process of dying. They are distinguished by the fact that first-degree euthanasia involves no medical treatment, whereas second-degree involves treatment—administered or withheld. There is a significant distinction within second-degree euthanasia as to whether treatment is administered or withheld—this is the distinction between what we will call the second stage and the first—but this is not the morally, ethically, and legally relevant distinction. That lies in intent, and that will appear within the boundaries of the second stage of second-degree euthanasia. It is important to note that this crucial change occurs within a second stage of a second degree, and thus may be obscure and very easy to overlook, because if it is overlooked, there will be nothing to stop dying from being widely anticipated by mercy killing, and—not too long thereafter—mercy killing to be supplemented by killing that no longer claims to be merciful, but merely useful. We distinguish the stages of second-degree euthanasia as follows:

a. Assistance in dying by withholding unnecessary, non-helpful treatment. This is medically, morally, and legally unobjectionable.

b. Assistance in dying by administration of therapy that has the anticipated but more or less unintended secondary effect of a more or less significant shortening of life. It is here—second degree, stage b—that the whole range of moral conduct, from innocence to guilt, is focused. In stage a—innocence; in stage c, guilt; in stage *b*, a difficult and crucial transition.

c. "Assistance in dying"—this time "assistance" in quotation marks—by administering medication to induce death. This is clearly killing, whether called "mercy" or not and, for the moment, is still criminal.

In considering the three stages of second-degree euthanasia, it is important to note that culpability is not primarily a question of the wishes of the patient. (In the foregoing situations, we should note that not only is a physician not culpable for not providing useless treatment, regardless of the wishes of the patient, but that it is actually unethical for him to do so. A surgeon should not agree to amputate a healthy limb or remove a healthy eye because a patient wishes to emulate Long John Silver or Moshe Dayan.) It is apparent that it is easy to glide, by imperceptible degrees, through the stages covered by "unintended although anticipated" to a "more" rather than a "less" significant shortening of life." To the extent that a death that would not ordinarily have occurred is induced by external means, one is dealing with homicide. Although it is possible for the stark dimensions of the question to be blurred, innocently or deliberately, by a mass of surrounding details, it is important to see the moral, ethical, and legal issue in full clarity.

Consider, for a moment, the question of a physician who shoots a terminally ill patient with a pistol—whether a Saturday-night special or a beautiful Smith & Wesson .357 Magnum. The physician's claim that the patient would have died in any event, within days or perhaps even hours, if he had not shot him, would hardly protect him from charges of homicide. If, instead of a pistol, the physician were to shoot his patient with a syringe filled with a lethal overdose of morphine, the moral, ethical, and legal issues would be identical, although the popular indignation would surely be less. Significant in both examples are the intent to kill and the fact that death was induced by the product administered—whether pharmaceutical or ballistic.

If we examine, for a moment, the case in which death is caused by an injection of morphine, we recognize that a wide variety of dosage is possible—from a quantity that will rapidly induce death at one end to a quantity that is too small to significantly alleviate pain at the other end of the scale. It is apparent that in the middle range of possible doses it becomes difficult to say what the anticipated and intended consequences must be. While other health care personnel can evaluate the probable effect of a particular dosage, namely, whether it will "more" or "less" significantly shorten life, no one but the administering physician himself can state whether the shortening is *intended* or merely *anticipated*.

This consideration shows that at a crucial point—and one that often is encountered in practice—the distinction between an unintentional shortening of life that cannot be called mercy killing and an intentional shortening of life that is mercy killing and is thus morally culpable if not easily indictable, lies in the heart, mind, and conscience of the physician, where it is not subject to third-party observation, supervision, or control.

Because the transition from a morally unobjectionable withholding of useless treatment (a), which ought not to be called mercy killing at all, to the potentially criminal use of medication to produce death (c), which is mercy killing pure and simple, passes through a cloudy region where the point of transition between morality and immorality, between innocence and culpability, may be totally impossible for the outside observer to discern, it is important for society to attempt to influence developments before this crucial point (b) is reached.

There are two ways in which such an influence can be exerted: first, in the training and ethical formation of health care personnel, in order that they can be expected, with reasonable confidence, to act with proper motives and intentions in circumstances (b). Second, it is in the interest of society to keep the distinctions between fundamentally different operations clear, by not permitting a morally unobjectionable procedure first to be labeled "passive euthanasia," then used as a lever to accustom the public to morally objectionable procedures of "active euthanasia," not excluding the third degree.

The dilemma of second-degree euthanasia reveals to us how difficult it is to legislate medical morality. We would not want a court or a legislature to prescribe medical treatment—how much worse to have it prescribing morality—yet morality is the crucial element. How can we guard it?

a. By exalting the principles. *Primum non nocere,* the physician's first duty is to do his patient no harm. The general principle does not solve every special case, but exalting it, proclaiming it, keeping it in mind, does help create an internal moral commitment.

b. By providing good examples. The ancient principle of authority: the ability to command voluntary obedience. Physicians need an inner spiritual formation—perhaps schools such as this can give it.

An Examination of Third-Degree Euthanasia

Mercy killing, as originally conceived and advocated, had to do only with those who were in the process of dying and who would shortly die, with or without medical treatment. To the extent that second-degree euthanasia becomes deliberate shortening of life, and, at its extreme limit, actual killing, its motivation frequently has expanded from concern for the *moriturus* to concern for those around him—family, dependents, those responsible for bearing the costs of his medical treatment, heirs and legatees, and finally society itself. In other words, a strong argument for the shortening of life becomes the cost of maintaining life. The final weeks and days of terminal care for a *moriturus* can be frighteningly expensive, but at least they have a natural term—the death of the patient. Unfortunately, there is a very large class of persons whose health care may not be as expensive as that provided a dying patient, but which ultimately can consume even greater amounts of money, time, and energy—precisely because they are not dying. Third-degree euthanasia involves the inducing of death among those who are not dying, but whose condition is such that someone—the patient himself, his dependents, or perhaps society at large can look on his death as "merciful," as a "release"—if not from suffering, then from onerous burdens and obligations. This class of persons is always very large and is capable of expansion at will. It is merely a question of definition. Let us consider some of the likeliest candidates for classification as persons whose death would bring "release."

a. Those suffering from irreversible brain damage, incapable of intelligent, sentient brain life: in vulgar parlance, vegetables. This class includes patients who can continue to "live" only if maintained on elaborate life-support equipment such as a respirator, as well as those who may take food and nourishment but give no evidence of intelligent mental awareness.

b. Those suffering from brain damage or mental impairment that seriously affects their intellectual potential: Down's syndrome patients, arteriosclerotic patients, idiots, morons; those suffering from physical handicaps that gravely impair their ability to function adequately, even given normal mental abilities: quadriplegics, victims of cerebral palsy, multiple sclerosis, blind, deaf, and dumb patients, paraplegic patients. It is apparent that stage b includes a wide range of individuals, running from those in whom mental life is virtually nonexistent to those in whom normal mental potential may be all but buried under physical impairments, to those whose mental and physical handicaps, while not overwhelming, are enough to cause a serious burden to them, to their families, and to society as a whole.

c. Persons whose lack of adjustment to society and to its demands make them troublesome and expensive: the criminally insane, habitual or repeating criminal offenders, vagabonds and malcontents. In this stage, it is again apparent that we are dealing with a broad range of individuals, some of whom may represent a continuing and severe threat to their fellow-humans, others of whom represent little more than a continual nuisance and expense.

d. Persons belonging to racial, ethnic, religious, or political groups that form or threaten to form a disturbing element in society. Here too one might be dealing with a wide range of possibilities, varying from committed criminal or terrorist groups such as the medieval Assassins, the dacoits of India, and the Mafia, through racial and ethnic minorities, to revolutionary political parties and members of enthusiastic or fanatical religious groups.

It is apparent that third-degree euthanasia, like second-degree, covers a range of activities that are quite different in nature and intent from one another. Members of groups (a) and (b) are, in general, innocent of any moral or legal offense. They are candidates for euthanasia partly because their lives are deemed worthless to them, either by themselves or, more frequently, by others who supposedly have their best interests at heart. In addition, they are, to varying degrees, a heavy burden on the resources of society and offer little or no promise of productive activity to offset their cost to society. They constitute a medical problem, inasmuch as they cannot survive at all without a considerable measure of costly medical attention, which is not available for other, perhaps more productive, members of society.

Members of groups (c) and (d) do not necessarily constitute a medical problem, nor are they necessarily a burden on the productivity of society. They may even be productive members of society in the course of their more or less legal activities. But they are deemed, by those with authority and responsibility, to constitute undesirable elements, elements whose social utility is less than their social cost. (In this connection, it is interesting to reflect on the assertion of advocates of zero population growth and of population reduction that human beings per se have negative environmental value, in that they burden the quality of the environment rather than improving it. By these standards, the whole human race could fall into the category of those whose cost exceeds their usefulness.)

Problems of Euthanasia

The topic of euthanasia presses itself upon us with intensity. As Prof. Paul Bernan wrote in *Grandeur et tentations de la médicine*, when he began medical practice in the 1920s, medicine was rather ineffective—but also inexpensive. Today it is much more effective—and vastly more expensive.

1. *The First Problem: The Hard Case.* As M. Clodius Sapiens, M.D., the brother of the learned jurist, put it, "Casus durus

morietur"—the hard case dies. But today, increasingly *casus durus vivit*. Because the hard cases are so numerous that they will overwhelm us, we must face the problem. Because they will cause us to make bad laws, we will have to put them aside and to try to consider principles.

2. *The Second Problem: The Bad Precedent.* Abortion has set the precedent for deciding hard cases on utilitarian grounds, on cost-effectiveness grounds. The next point has to do with similarities that show that what we have decided in abortion may be transferred to euthanasia. If abortion is a bad precedent, euthanasia is another.

3. *The Usurpation of Another's Moral Right.* If anyone has the right to determine whether a life is worth living, it certainly should be the person himself. Abortion usurps that right, in the name of maternal health, wantedness, or "quality of life." If abortion for these reasons is accepted—and it is—and found moral, even praiseworthy, as some do and others are not astute enough to notice—then surely euthanasia at the subject's request—voluntary euthanasia—must be acceptable. And where the subject is unable to make such a decision, others will make it for him. This is already being done. What about the situation where the subject is *able,* but unwilling—this is certainly not far in the future.

4. *The Slippery Slide.* Euthanasia presents us with "hard case law" based on utilitarian considerations, considerations of cost-effectiveness. It is a logical consequence of abortion (and infanticide). It accustoms us to the usurpation of the rights of others, at first often (ostensibly) for their own good, later for our economy and convenience. These grounds can lead us through the stages of second-degree euthanasia to true "mercy killing" and then to the third degree, killing for convenience.

Proposals

How are we to confront the steady march of both medical "ethics" and of law and public policy from "spiritual euthanasia" through mercy killing properly so-called to "euthanasia" as a euphemism for killing for convenience? It is necessary to approach the problem on several different levels: pastoral, medical, and legal.

Pastoral Proposals. Speaking both as a pastor and to others involved in the pastorate, in church-related education, and in Christian counseling, I appeal first of all for three spiritual and educational initiatives, and then for the provision of a practical alternative to point the way to escape what otherwise seems an irresistible drift towards killing as the "treatment of choice" for a multitude of problems—medical, financial, and social.

First, it is important to accustom—or re-accustom—people to the idea that death, although "the last enemy" (1 Cor 15:26) and not a natural part of life, as the death-with-dignity school would have it, is nevertheless man's inescapable temporal destiny: "It is given to men once to die, and after this, the judgment" (Heb 9:27). Be prepared for it, and, even more important, prepare yourself and others. The early Christians were well aware of the need to prepare for death—no doubt because the Romans were so eager to drag Christians off to the arena and throw them to the lions.

Specifically, we should teach our families and those around us to know what we want done and not done if we are overtaken by an irreversible, terminal sickness and can no longer make our wishes known. We must also encourage them, individually, to make their wishes known, if possible to get them so thoroughly on record with family members and physicians that no one will be in any doubt concerning their wishes if they were to lose the ability to communicate them. Having done this, we should take a stand on—usually against—the many proposals and some laws concerning "living wills," "natural death," and "death with dignity." Some of them are plausible, and many are superficially unobjectionable, even valuable, but all of them are dangerous—which is why the euthanasia advocates so strongly support them. What we need is not a death-with-dignity-bill, nor a living-will-bill. These bills do not permit a physician to do or refrain from doing anything that is not permitted already. What they in fact do is to give a sensation of comfort on the one hand, while on the other paving the way for true third-stage, second-degree euthanasia and beyond. What each of us needs as an individual is not a living will, but a responsible Christian physician—or other physician committed to Hippocratic principles—whom he can trust and on whom he can rely to do the correct, the compassionate, and the moral thing if and when he lies on his deathbed beneath the doctor's hands.

In addition to accustoming people not yet patients to the thought that someday they must die, it is also important to accustom physicians to the idea. I hope that those who are physicians do not find this suggestion impertinent from a non-physician. It is self-evident that everyone in medical practice, as in the ministry, has to deal with death and with the reality that people, even the patients of good doctors, die. Yet I believe that I can observe that many physicians find it very difficult to deal with the death of a patient. My father was a physician; immediately after his death, his own doctor—a younger colleague—disappeared, speaking neither to my mother, nor to me, nor to anyone else. There was no further contact. From pastoral experience I know that this man is far from the only physician who finds it difficult to deal with the situation that arises when a patient actually dies. Just as pastors sometimes need others to reassure them that in the last analysis they are not personally responsible for the salvation of their parishoners, so physicians sometimes need to be reassured that they are not responsible for the "latter end" of the dying patient.

A third important area of pastoral responsibility is this: families must be exhorted and taught to show love and concern before patients are in the last stages of a fatal illness. It so often happens that when an old relative, neglected and ignored for years, lies dying, the family suddenly rallies and tells her doctor, "Do all that you can to save her, doctor: she means so much to us." And thus a dying aunt, neglected in life, is placed on all sorts of elaborate equipment and spends her final days and hours in very expensive unconsciousness. It would have been far better for her nieces and nephews, instead of suddenly being overcome by guilt feelings when she lay at the point of death, to have loved her and ministered to her during her lifetime, when she could have appreciated it.

Finally, because of the disappearance of the large family and for a variety of other sociological and economic reasons, it is vitally important for pastors to seek out or seek to establish a network of Christian hospices, where terminal patients can be given care and comfort, spiritual and natural euthanasia, and where they need not fear, when the doctor goes to his black bag, that he will pull out the .357 magnum.

Medical Proposals. My medical proposals parallel those given by my former teacher, George Williams, in his own presentation. We need a conscious recovery of the Hippocratic-Christian ethic. It is astonishing how rapidly this ethic, in use for over two millennia and dominant for almost that long, has been eroded in recent years. We can contribute to this by discussion and education, by constantly appealing to physicians and to the whole health care profession to remember the principles that truly made medicine a healing art. Of course, non-physicians—"laymen," in the medical vernacular—can do only so much towards this goal. The fundamental steps need to be taken by health care professionals themselves.

A first step might be the establishment of a kind of Hippocratic guild—perhaps not so different from the original school that gathered around Hippocrates—of physicians dedicated to the reformation of medical ethics. In the course of time, patients would come to recognize the existence of a class of physicians who could be trusted to act in accordance with the Judeo-Christian, Hippocratic ethic. (It is a remarkable thing that with over one hundred medical schools in the United States, there is no individual school or medical faculty, thus far, that has distinguished itself by taking a stand for those principles to which all were giving lip service less than a generation ago. The supine collaboration of German physicians in Hitler's various programs of extermination becomes more understandable, if not more commendable, in the light of our own medical educators' reluctance to take a stand for any of the traditional values of medicine.)

A second step is the creation and endowment, as well as the protection, of Christian medical schools. There are a number of Roman Catholic medical faculties in this country, as well as some overseas. The only one with a distinctively evangelical Protestant orientation is Oral Roberts University, the sponsor of our present conference. Nevertheless, each of these Christian-oriented schools must concentrate so hard on earning and maintaining a place of respect in the fiercely competitive world of modern medicine that—pardon me if ignorance causes me to slight anyone—not even these schools have been able to take a marked stand for Christian, Hippocratic principles. Rather than being Christians who self-consciously practice medicine as Christians, they seem to be physicians and scientists who incidentally and to varying degrees practice Christianity.

If the present Christian-oriented faculties are to become more committed to a self-consciously Christian approach in medicine, and if new institutions are to arise to stand with them, we must be realistic about the fact that such institutions will begin to draw the ire of much of the existing medical establishment, and of government as well. Hannah Arendt, in *The Origins of Totalitarianism,* states that one fundamental step towards totalitarianism is the creation of the atomistic mass. This atomistic mass is characterized by the fact that it no longer contains self-confident, self-conscious groups committed to their own distinctive ideals. To paraphrase Carlyle, bureaucracy standardizes, and absolute bureaucracy standardizes absolutely. Our own government, the relatively benign socialism of Sweden, and the fiercely repressive "socialism" of the Soviet Union all have in common a distaste, verging on detestation, for any groups or parties with a distinctive ethic, one they are willing to defend.

A third step—and one within the reach of many institutions represented at this gathering—is the creation and funding of chairs and institutes for the development and application of a Christian ethic in medicine and in other biomedical areas. Consider the tremendous—and baleful—influence of a single teacher, Dr. Joseph Fletcher, who followed his career as a teacher of future ministers in the Episcopal Theological School (Cambridge, Massachusetts) with an appointment at the University of Virginia Medical School. Fletcher was able to exercise a very significant influence on the future course of medical ethics by virtue of the fact that for a number of years he was virtually alone in the expression of his radical proposals for the demolition of traditional Hippocratic, Judeo-Christian ethics in medicine. There is no comparable platform in any American medical school—and this is surely not because there is no conservative Roman Catholic or evangelical Protestant thinker of equal status.

There are two famous institutes working in the area of medical ethics, the Hastings Institute and the Kennedy Institute; unfortunately, both of them seem to be more attuned to the spirit of the age than to the Holy Spirit. The Christian Action Council, in Washington, D.C., which takes a very clear Judeo-Christian line with regard to medical and biomedical ethics, has recently been joined in the nation's capital by the American Center for Bioethics, which hopes to bring a more distinctively Christian kind of thinking to bear on problems in biomedical ethics.

Legal Proposals. Earlier in our presentation, it may have been suggested, at least implicitly, that many health care professionals are culpably abandoning the Hippocratic ethic. That this is happening is undeniable, but to some extent it is understandable. Physicians have been and increasingly are being subjected to frivolous, vicious, and exploitative malpractice claims and suits. Many members of the medical profession appear scared to death by the imminent danger to fortune, if not to life, that threatens them at every moment from unjustified or marginally justifiable malpractice charges. There was a time when the internal solidarity of the medical profession routinely rejected all or virtually all malpractice charges, so that it was difficult, if not impossible, to hold a physician responsible even for marked negligence and professional irresponsibility. In Europe, malpractice suits are virtually unknown, except in the rare case where a physician has acted in such a way as to make himself not merely civilly but criminally liable. This ever-present threat, now swollen to grotesque proportions, causes all but the most courageous physicians to take self-protective measures that often are neither in accordance with traditional ethics nor in the best interest of their patients. Legal protection must be restored to physicians engaged in conscientious practice according to the best current standards of their calling. At the same time, it is necessary for physicians as a profession to exercise more responsible self-control.

A step towards ending the specter of unjustified and frivolous malpractice claims would be the reaffirmation of the propriety of withholding treatment when treatment would be useless. The old medical ethic taught that the physician ought never to administer useless or harmful treatment. It is this duty, or rather the right to fulfill it, that the living will and similar proposals seek to protect. We must find a way to achieve this goal without plunging down the slippery slope towards which the living will is intended to direct us.

The legal profession and the legislatures must work to avoid all "slippery slope" enactments, and especially laws that gradually, consciously or unconsciously, lead into "third-stage" euthanasia and thence into plain killing.

Finally, as the medical profession must seek to reaffirm the Hippocratic ethic and pastors to recover the biblical perspective on death, the law must return to the old—and valid—American understanding of the source of life and of the meaning of the right to life. In my own high school days, we were taught the slogan—as part of the American tradition—that each human life is of infinite value. Even in high school, before taking any courses in philosophy or theology, I was able to figure out that such a claim overstates the case: no finite being—and finite is what each of us is—can have infinite value.

Unfortunately, from that assertion—which, although exaggerated, was not particularly dangerous—we have suddenly tumbled into the opposite, the assertion that each human life is of no value. Indeed, advocates of Zero Population Growth and of Negative Population Growth will tell us that human lives are of negative value—they pollute the environment more than they enhance it. A legal corrective to this view was offered by the West German Supreme Court (*Bundesverfassungsgericht*) in its abortion decision of February 1975. In contrast to our own Supreme Court in *Roe v. Wade,* the West German court began by reaffirming the axiom that every human life is a subject with rights, which it is the duty of the law to defend, if necessary even against the wishes of the mother. It cannot always be defended, and there are circumstances, according to the West German decision, in which abortion cannot be forbidden. Nevertheless, the developing human being in the womb is precisely that—a human being—and the law has the duty to protect it. This is a principle that United States law not merely does not recognize, but actively opposes. The United States Constitution, testifies abortion strategist Harriet Pilpel, does not contain a right to life. She is right; it does not, but it ought to. Placing this most fundamental of all human rights, the right to life, in our Constitution is a first-class challenge to the stewards of the law.

Pastors, physicians, lawyers—professionals in their own fields, "laymen" to one another—do not have sole power or responsibility to shape our values in this important area where life itself is at stake. But as professionals their power is greater, their influence is greater, and their responsibility is heavier. Each of us should do as Moses advised the children of Israel when he left them on the banks of the Jordan:

"Choose life, that ye may live, ye and your children" (Dt 30:19, paraphrased).

SEVEN

Decisions for Death
and the Law

by Walter Probert

T HE SORT OF LIFE OR DEATH DECISIONS that arise in the care of
critically ill or terminal patients have not brought easy
answers from the legal system. Any truly considered attempt to
set forth the law which applies at once produces the persistent
puzzle of jurisprudential theory—just what phenomena qualify
as law anyway? Indeed there are few of the significant
jurisprudential issues that do not rise up to tangle rational
analysis in this area, especially the issue of the relation betwen
law and morality.

Legal positivists tend to find law mostly in the articulations of
sovereign authority, constitutions, statutes, and judicial opinions.[1] Such law is scant here. Yet we may comfortably project
the law of the nation from but a few authorities if we recognize
the law as perhaps developing more on the informal level, in the
hospitals as much as in the formal organs of state such as
legislatures and courts.[2] At least that is the situation regarding
decisions to withhold life-prolonging treatment from incompetent patients.[3]

On the other hand, the law regarding competent patients has
more of formality about it. Courts have so far made it clear that
under most circumstances yet tested, a competent patient has

the right to refuse medical intervention, even if it is life prolonging.[4] Yet in another sense, this part of the law relevant to our topic is at best but deference to the sovereignty of the competent patient, at worst an abdication to private law-making. Moral law is not controlling of judicial decision in those situations which fall short as clear examples of homicide or suicide.

There is, all the same, one kind of moral premise involved in the judicial response. Implicit is an evaluation of the relative importance of individual self-determination as against the coercive power of health care agents. Courts have supported if not generated an allocation of power away from physicians to patients. That allocation is clearly apparent and generally morally justifiable where the patient's life is not at stake.[5]

In those situations we speak in both ethical and legal discourse of informed consent. Under that theory, the physician's judgment of what is best for the patient is not controlling. What the patient decides and what information he is legally and morally entitled to is not a medical question in the scientific or technological sense, nor in the sense of the sometimes circumscribed ethics of the medical profession.

A requirement of informed consent is a great step for democratic values, but the next steps are not necessarily all for the good in the preservation of overriding moral values. Informed consent relates to the patient's decision whether to accede to an operation, diagnostic tests, drug therapy, or whatever treatment, in or out of critical care. The next step is to protect a competent patient in his refusal of life-saving or life-prolonging medical intervention. The further next step is to protect incompetent patients against such intervention—or more subtly, their caretakers in their decisions to veto such intervention.

Entangled with these decisions are serious questions for both law and ethics on definitions of life and death and living and dying. We had no great problem with these definitions not so very long ago. The price of medical progress is a tragic gray area in which quality of life becomes the determinant, hidden behind subtle distinctions and clumsy definitions common to the rhetoric of both lawyers and ethicists.[6] Changing social dynamics and technology always produce changing laws or else tensions between law and society. In this instance, medical capacities to save and prolong life have outstripped our formal laws and maybe our legal machinery.

Perhaps we are in the process of changing our definitions of life, or of life worth preserving. Maybe we may do so morally, and so legally. We surely need help in that vision. There needs to be more public awareness of these issues than there has been. Private law-making and value-making in the hospital, the hospice, and the nursing home may leave too much to the faith of humanism. Yet the courts are not really fitted to the task.

Judicial Trial and Error

The response of the formal agencies of the legal process to the problems of life or death in critical and terminal care has been mostly judicial. There has been legislative action in legitimating medical definitions of brain death and, more questionably, in attempting to legitimate decisions for death in advance of incompetency.[7] If legislation is desirable in this area at this time, it may be to place a limit on questionable judicial decisions. As is generally true, judicial development has been trial and error in response to randomly arising situations. The results are mixed.

On the positive side, the courts have remained accessible to give answers and provide guidance in disputed life or death situations. In other areas of concern, disputes are usually judicially resolved in claims for damages, or wrong decisions are reviewed in prosecutions for crime—as they may be here. In other health care situations, physicians or patients do not come to court to ask whether diagnoses or operations are legally acceptable. They rarely have done so in the life or death situations. Yet decisions on that level are very different. Decisions for death moot review so far as the patient is concerned. Certainly if there is disagreement, there needs to be some arena for resolution. Some observers believe there should be judicial review even in the absence of disagreement, if there is a decision for death, at least in the case of an incompetent.[8] So far, the courts are the only available formal agency.

Another positive note; we are beginning to see a legal legitimation or charting of areas of discretion: (1) for the competent patient in his decision on life-supporting or life-prolonging medical intervention; (2) for physicians in what are inevitably within the medical province in the no-coding of terminal patients;[9] (3) for caretakers of incompetent patients in withholding of treatment or life support.

However, in conjunction with this sort of helpful judicial response, there are some worrisome developments. Most generally, there does seem to be an erosion of the sanctity of life as a value in law. While debate on the morality of abortion continues, the impact of permissive abortion on that value surely cannot be questioned. Perhaps it has had an impact on the other end of the life spectrum. Indeed, one court has strongly urged the analogy.[10] Permissive dying—a limited right to die or let die—has been rested on the same constitutional base as permissive abortion, the right of privacy.[11] It is without doubt a seamless web.

The Worrisome Spring *Case*

Massachusetts is at once the crucible state and the forum of the most worrisome decision to date, the *Spring* case involving an incompetent.[12] Its potential impact is somewhat obscured by the diversity of its issues: (1) Should judicial authorization be required for withdrawal of life-support treatment? (2) To what extent are medical standards or practices controlling? (3) What should be the role of familial caretakers?

Earl Spring was 79 years old, irreversibly senile, and suffering loss from an "end stage" kidney disease. Survival was dependent upon thrice weekly dialysis preceded by sedation to overcome his resistance to the therapy. According to the court, he had a possible life expectancy of five years. His wife and son petitioned for and received judicial authorization to withhold further dialysis.

The rationale of the case was cast in terms of the right of the patient to reject treatment, via the substituted judgment of his wife and son. Conceivably the decision may generate out of court decisions in which economic and emotional impact on the family are in fact the major determinants. However physicians may view such a potential, the more important feature of the case to them is likely to be that it marked a judicial withdrawal from the stance of an earlier decision which was most unpopular in medical circles.

That was the *Saikewicz* case.[13] Involved was an incompetent resident of a state institution who was suffering from terminal leukemia. While of advanced years, his mental capacity was at the two-year level. The court authorized the withholding of chemotherapy which at best had a short-range life-prolonging potential. The *Saikewicz* opinion was interpreted as holding that judicial authority was obligatory in any situation involving the withholding of life-support or of life-prolonging therapy from an incompetent patient.

If, as some lawyers and physicians believed, that affected no-code practices, the subsequent *Dinnerstein* case[14] cleared the air. It in effect legitimated the kind of medical discretionary control that is almost inescapably associated with patients for whom death is imminent. The *Spring* case then made it clear that unless a state institution was involved with no familial caretaker, then judicial authorization was not required.[15] There was a caveat issued, however: while the decision to withhold treatment was not required to be judicially previewed, such a decision was necessarily reviewable in a possible criminal prosecution. In such an event, the question would be whether the decision to withhold involved a good faith effort to follow accepted medical standards.

There may not in fact be medical standards covering such situations, unless the general practice be to defer to the preference of the familial caretakers.[16] Surely the question is not a purely medical one. Thus the medical profession is being invested with a kind of law-making power. The court denied that quality of life considerations could be relevant in its decision, yet they most assuredly would be among those factors considered by the physician and relevant family members. In short, the court deferred to the ethics of the caretakers, medical and familial.

How, then, did we come this far?

The Freedom of the Competent Person to Die

It all starts with each person's legal right to be free of harmful or even offensive bodily contacts, i.e., intended intrusions, among others, medical interventions. In emergencies, when a person is unable to give or deny consent to medical treatment, consent is "implied" on the reasonable basis that each person is presumed to prefer as healthy a life as possible.[17] Otherwise, the competent person is sovereign, an autonomous, self-determining being, legally entitled to decide his own fate,[18] to weigh the pros and cons of life with recommended treatment or without, even of life as against death.

Further, he is entitled to reasonably adequate information as the basis of his choice. The requirement of informed consent[19] comes from a moral perspective regarding the dignity and freedom of the human being. To some extent it has been imposed against medical ethics. Thus, the right to refuse life-saving or life-prolonging treatment is but a dramatic instance of the more general right. It is based on the interest of the individual which courts have come to regard as superior to that which physicians may have to promote health over sickness, improvement even if not cure, life over death. It is not the judgment of the physician as to the best interest of the patient; it is the judgment of the patient which prevails, right or wrong.

It would be better to refer to the person's freedom to be wrong.[20] Calling it a right to refuse could lead to calling it a right to die. Some judicial opinions have based this freedom on the constitutional right of privacy,[21] bringing unavoidable comparisons with *Roe v. Wade.*[22] However that case has since been interpreted, it did not articulate a right to an abortion, but a right to be free of state intervention, the freedom to decide in favor of abortion, even if it is morally wrong.[23] In that strict sense, the competent person does not have a right to die in any absolute sense—not yet. Even so, he has a limited right to die if his circumstances place him in the situation where he may die by refusal of treatment.

Thus do we see the further point of the decline in the law's reenforcement of the sanctity of life.[24] The individual is entitled to let himself die rather than experience or suffer an unwanted treatment or an unacceptable life process. We must wonder how long the line can be held against a building pressure to give legal protection to a right to die by affirmative action. The point does come when in an individual situation the moral and legal distinction between active and passive is simply not maintainable and maybe even unjust. Maybe there is need to reexamine the possible limit of the "right of refusal."[25] Of course there is an understandable judicial apprehension of coercion on some medical rack and a correlative appreciation that there needs to be some limit to legal coercion. In that sense there is involved deference to the moral dynamics of our society. If so, then the cure may not be in tightening the law but in improving the moral climate and the decision-making system in the hospital. To say, for instance, that a person has the freedom to refuse treatment does not mean that physicians may not under appropriate circumstances initiate various means of moral suasion against a decision for death. Indeed under some circumstances surely a physician has a moral duty to make the attempt, maybe even a legal duty.

How to Decide for the Incompetent

The conception of the competent person as a free moral, self-determining individual has not reached but it is approaching the absolute position formerly held by the conception of the sanctity of life. Of course the legally incompetent person cannot be perceived in that way for his lack of mental or physical capacity to reason or to communicate. Yet, generally speaking, as a person his being is still thought morally and legally worthy of protection. He has rights, including some degree of a right to medical treatment. However, to some extent his rights must be promoted by proxy, often by a legally appointed guardian. In the case of life or death decisions, the incompetent person's freedom to reject treatment could be exercised or supervised by some sort of agency of the state. The only presently authorized agency is the judiciary.

The leading case involved Karen Ann Quinlan.[26] Her bare life expectancy presumably depended on what was styled as the extraordinary means of a respirator such that if it was removed she would die. The court equated her right with that of competent persons. The right was hers, to be exercised on her behalf by her father as guardian, in this instance to reject further medical intervention. The alternative would have been for the court to mandate continued life support or to apply a set of criteria which would in this or some instance justify cessation of life support, inevitably involving a determination that some lives need not be maintained at all costs.

The *Quinlan* case was a strong one for the use of the substituted judgment test.[27] Nonetheless, it is important to consider whether there is any way that test can be used without masking important value judgments, including quality of life sorts of measurements. Short of some timely written statement signed by Karen Quinlan herself, there was inevitably a moral kind of judgment involved. It was not Karen who was exercising her right; it was her father who was exercising his judicially legitimated power, immune from any sort of legal liability, so long as no prevailing medical standard was violated. To say he is not guilty of homicide is to follow the now accepted moral and legal position. It is a moral judgment that the life should not be prolonged. If it were a life that it was believed should be prolonged, then to withhold life-prolonging treatment would be homicide because it would involve a violation of a duty to the patient.

From *Quinlan* in New Jersey we move to *Spring* in Massachusetts by the steps previously traced. Against that background, it seems almost inevitable that nationally the formal law, whether by legislation or judicial response, will in the irreversible coma situation of the *Quinlan* case legalize caretaker withholding of life support.[28] Even more clearly, the formal law nationally will coincide with the unwritten law of the hospital in legitimating no code decisions when a person is in fact in the process of dying. The rationale is that there is no duty to prolong dying. In the *Quinlan* situation, there is no duty to prevent a person from dying when that person is all but dead in a strictly legal sense.

The *Saikewicz* situation calls for a different approach. To say that the substituted judgment approach can be used for a person who has never advanced beyond infancy in mentality is of course fiction, potentially a risky if not a dangerous fiction.[29] It falls closer to the situation of the malformed infant.[30] Since there was no caring relative, judicial intervention was and should be mandated. It is not just a medical question whether such a person should be coerced into a possibly worse life experience solely for the sake of prolonging it. Perhaps it is a judgment that anyone would make to cease treatment. But such cases serve as precedent for decisions that are less clear. There is an ethical question which should be subject to public scrutiny and potential debate.

Had there been a caring relative in the *Saikewicz* situation then it would come closer to Earl Spring's situation. It would still be true that substituted judgment would not be possible *vis à vis* Saikewicz, the mental retardate.[31] In the Earl Spring situation, substituted judgment is at least thinkable. However, absent any clear previous expression of preference on the part of Spring, there is simply no way to guarantee that the caretakers are not thinking mainly or purely in their own interest. Indeed it is predictable that they would. If such a life needs to be prolonged for the sake of preserving the sanctity of life generally, then perhaps the relatives should have a right to free themselves of that burden, but not necessarily by a "passive abortion." Perhaps the interests of the state and of society can and ought to be protected by the assumption of at least the economic burden. That mere suggestion, of course, will raise utilitarian opposition.

In any event, there should not be the kind of deference to medical practice and "ethics" that is manifested in the *Spring* opinion. It is not purely a medical question, clearly, whether it is right to let the person die. It is a moral question of great moment! Surely it is not the sort of moral question which only physicians can or should answer.

In the *Quinlan* case, the court suggested the desirability of an Ethics Committee to review the decision for death.[32] Such an agency has not been legally mandated anywhere. Some such approach is needed, preferably in dynamics not dominated by physicians. Every hospital should articulate guidelines and mandate procedures for at least unofficial review in counseling-like sessions. The idea is that moral constraints must have an opportunity to influence the decision. The need is not so much for a legal agency like a court to review the decisions, but a moral agency, perhaps an Ethics Consortium for the Protection of Human Life.[33] Its mission would be to determine when it is both morally and legally acceptable to act on behalf of the patient to reject further medical intervention, so as not to prolong useless suffering, inhumane conditions, and so on. Clear evidence that the patient would not have wanted medical intervention would be relevant, although not necessarily determinative. The patient should not have to be terminal to justify cessation of medical intervention, but if he is not, then there ought be be a moral presumption against it. The *Spring* case is worrisome because there seemed to be a presumption in favor of death.

Conclusion

We are inching ever closer to a utilitarian approach in life or death decisions for persons who are terminal or who are critically ill or severely disabled, so far as a judgment regarding life-prolonging medical intervention is involved. The competent person is free to base his decision on almost any ground he chooses. That premise sets the base for the incompetent's situation. So long as he is attended by a qualified physician and represented by a person who has been intimately related to him, then the potential looming ahead is that they may decide to withhold treatment on the same grounds as might influence a decision by a competent person. We are not there yet, but the prospect seems inevitable.

The outer legal limit seems really to be that there shall be no active intervention to end a person's life. Courts are not apt to shift that line in the foreseeable future. It seems possible that social attitudes may eventually support such a move. The line presently seems to hold less out of concern for requiring a particular person to live than for concern that there is no sure way to hold any other line against unjustified homicides.

Courts will and must maintain their role to preserve the rights of both the competent and the incompetent. They will also maintain their role of protector of social values where those are clearly established, e.g., in a prosecution for unjustified homicide.

Whatever any one of us may feel or even know about the morality of withholding medical treatment, courts are not appropriate agencies in our pluralistic society to choose among competing values of such complexity as are involved here. This writer's view is that physicians are not either. Whether decision-making should be left more or less at the private level in the case of incompetents is now a public issue. Conceivably institutional review agencies could be legislatively mandated. It seems more likely that we will see them spring up in random fashion under increasing public pressure, as much for institutional self-protection as for concern for the preservation of so much of the sanctity of life as yet remains. No matter, they will serve that function as well.

Under such accumulating public experience, the time may come when we will be more ready than we are now to articulate the freedoms and the limits.

EIGHT

"Safer Footing than Blind Reason Stumbling Without Fear"

Reflections on Bioethics in Our Civic, Religious, Historical, Professional Context

George Huntston Williams

Dedicated to my sister-in-law and my brother, Dr. Polesta Iwanaga and Dr. David Cator Williams, who though not wholly in agreement with my points have long served as compassionate physicians in Cleveland and Bay Village, Ohio.

I. Introduction

We are brought from the perspectives of law, medicine, and theology to discuss in often taxing detail legal and moral problems that arise with special reference to four selected topics: abortion and contraception, amniocentesis, infanticide, and euthanasia. Amid such discussions, as a church historian, I can only make a contribution as a concerned observer of the larger context of highly professional papers and as one who has sought to understand the historical development which has brought us together seeking clarification and consensual direction.

My title might have been "Bioethics in the Sacred Condominium," but in resorting instead to a line from Shakespeare, I wished to sound a note of caution. It is true that we can become too fearful at the brinks of scientific discovery. My own Harvard University found itself at the center of intense controversy in 1976 over the specter of an Andromeda Strain of bacteria escaping from the DNA-Recombitant Center with the mayor of Cambridge and a Nobel laureate in biology sounding the alarm.[1] Although fear has indeed interfered with the scientific advances, there is a ruthlessness in every profession in the pursuit of goals that take on an imperative of their own; and it is indeed to the credit of the medical profession and allied disciplines that they have sought the counsel of outsiders, still intending to uphold the principle, to use a phrase from Lucian of Samosata, "that no commands should be put upon a holy calling, taught by the gods and exercised by men of learning; moreover, it [their practice] should not be subject to enslavement by the law. . . . The physician ought to be persuaded, not ordered."[2]

In classical antiquity physicians often constituted a guild, and they practiced medicine and surgery as a right, not as a privilege. They were governed not by laws of the state but rather by codes of their guild or school. The School of Hippocrates was such a guild, and in many respects an exception in its practices, more consonant with what would become eventually Christian usage in the realm of healing. As guilds developed in the towns of the Latin Middle Ages, physicians again became organized in guilds; but licensure was introduced as medicine became a university discipline. Medicine was henceforth practiced as a privilege, not as a right. Moreover, canonical and moral casuists began to prepare manuals of proper norms of conscience for the guidance of priests dealing with the sins of commission and omission disclosed in the confessional in relation to various professionals, including physicians and surgeons.[3] The confessional was the penitential tribunal with its *ius poli* of the internal, secret *forum*, in contrast to the judication of the external tribunal, the *forum externum*.

In his counsel for priests in the confessional, Bartholomaeus Fumus in his *Summa Armilla* (Cologne, 1538) warned of the rashness of physicians eager to learn more or unwilling to acknowledge ignorance: "[W]hen ignorance of the ailment but from *rashness* or lest they be thought to be ignorant, or for the sake of gain, they undertake to treat the patient, exposing him to the danger of death, or of notable harm, this is mortal sin."[4] In still undivided Latin Christendom theologians thus constrained physicians. Yet we know how often even today this fear of "rashness" on the part of professionals has actually also impeded important research.

It will have been my primary contribution to show how, against an historical background, we should be seeking to descry the outlines and the modalities of something in our time that combines the features of the internal and the external forum, that preserves the integrity of the profession of medicine, while finding in its ethical practice in healing and research a proper place for the concerns of society at large and of the patients and their kin, of all patients from conception to natural death. This evolving institution must go beyond the local hospital review board or ethics committee. More and more now "law is being made in the hospitals."[5] The theory of such deliberations must be thought through and provided with collegial support and legislative authorization and regularized oversight from outside the hospital and laboratory. I will be calling this new kind of forum for the New Biology *the sacred condominium*. It would give institutional embodiment to diverse claims and considerations, none of which may be left out of account, but which are likely to suffer neglect under some existing practices and professional attitudes and the inability of statutory law to keep abreast of medical advances. Within this deliberative forum of several shifting co-sovereignties dealing with what we have come to regard as sacred—human life—the problems of bioethics, which I define as *micro*bioethics, should never be isolated from ethical considerations pressing upon us from what I would, in contrast, call *macro*bioethics, the morality of public medicine in the broadest context: the global perspective I will make clearer at the end (Part VI) for how this sacred condominium could resolve differences between the general public, represented in part by the law, and the medical and the new microbial sciences.

My enigmatic title from Shakespeare, amid all the straight-forward titles of the program, is from the speech of Cressida, daughter of a Trojan priest who cast his lot with the besieging Greeks. Left in the care of a frivolous and scheming uncle, Cressida herself is a winsome and witty flirt amidst the fortunes of war. It is the Trojan king's son Troilus of whom she is first enamored that she says, with wisdom far above the immediate peril to her life, love, and destiny: "Blind fear, that seeing reason leads, finds safer footing than blind reason stumbling without fear. To fear the worst oft cures the worse."[6] Shakespeare is only with reservation to be called an Elizabethan Christian. The fact that his language and style is similar to the King James version of the Bible, authorized at about the time *Troilus and Cressida* (1609) was printed, should not mislead us to assume that his thought was biblical. His plays, however, embody much that we should call wisdom in the observation of the human condition. Shakespearean scholars hold that this satirical comedy was first played not in the often rowdy Globe Theatre but rather in a chamber of one of the Inns of Court before sophisticated barristers and solicitors on some festive occasion. Cressida said something wise for a law school sponsoring a seminar on bioethics: "To fear the worst oft cures the worse," for we are surely dealing with difficult dilemmas; and reason illumined can help us as lawyers, doctors, ethicists, and other professionals find our way amid the perils of our day lest we stumble into awesome catastrophes for the human race because we lack the prudence and self-discipline instilled by fear; for "the fear of the Lord is the beginning of wisdom" (Prv 1:17).

II. The Origin of the Term "Bioethics" and Divergent Emphasis in Its Use

"Bioethics" is not yet in the dictionaries.

The International Military Tribunal at Nuremberg, with the help of physicians, prepared the Nuremberg Code with special reference to experiments on human beings.[7] In July 1981 Robert J. Lifton, on the basis of interviews with ninety-three S.S. doctors of the death camps, gave a paper, "The Medicalization of Auschwitz," observing that the man who made the fateful decisions, as he moved among the boxcarloads of deportees, wore a white orderly's uniform, that the keg of Zyklon Pellets brought by train was carried in a Red Cross ambulance with two medics accompanying it to the "bathhouses."[8]

The Declaration of Geneva of 1948 of the World Medical Association, reflecting outrage at the behavior of Nazi doctors, was an oath modeled on that of Hippocrates but updated so as not to "permit considerations of religion, nationality, race, party politics or social standing . . . even under threat" to induce the doctor to act "contrary to the laws of humanity . . . while maintaining utmost respect for human life, from the time of conception."[9] Later, the World Medical Association, in the framework of the International Code of Medical Ethics, adopted the evolved Declaration of Helsinki in 1964 as a guide to doctors in clinical research. Thus in consequence of the deeds in the laboratories of concentration camps of the university profession most carried away by Nazi racist and eugenicist indoctrination, namely, the medical profession, the core of the Helsinki Declaration combines in its second paragraph an affirmation from the Declaration of Geneva, "The health of my patient will be my first consideration," with an admonition from the International Code of Medical Ethics, "Any act or advice which could weaken physical or mental resistance of a human being may be used only in his interest."

In 1968 the World Council of Churches convened near Geneva (Bossey) an ecumenical consultation to deal specifically with experiments on man. The assembled specialists, including persons whose churches are not members of the Council, like Professor Edmund D. Pellegrino, S.J., now president of Catholic University of America, broke up into three working parties. One of these, called upon to revise The Declaration of Helsinki with concerns appropriate to Christian physicians, was headed by the Unitarian cancer scholar of the University of Wisconsin, Professor Van Rensselaer Potter. The reworked and much expanded Christian modification of The Helsinki Declaration constitutes part one of the edited findings.[10] The entire consultation elaborated the beginnings of "an ethic for bio-ethical research and practice, . . . and in so doing set forth five possible 'theological approaches,' " which the report acknowledged "were mentioned and partly discussed," but evidently did not inform the findings.

In 1971 Unitarian Potter published his *Bioethics: Bridge to the Future* (Englewood Cliffs, N.J.: Prentice-Hall) and Catholic Andre Hellegers (d. May 1979) became at Georgetown University the Director of the Kennedy Institute for Human Reproduction and Bioethics. Thus "bioethics" appeared in 1971 and in quite different contexts. The manipulation at the level of microbiology is hard for all but the specialists to visualize, grasp, and possibly to feel passionate or even compassionate about, though no one can remain other than awed in the presence of such a wondrous realm and state of being called life. The essential difference between Potter's use of the word, the first in print,[11] and Helleger's is that in the first instance there is an optimism about the possibilities of auto-evolution and human progress, while in the second instance there is a stress not so much on doing good as on not doing harm. Progress and restraint are the two contrasting dispositions. Moreover, the originator of the term in Madison emphatically places bioethics in the context of environmental ethics. The restraint in Georgetown is there because of a long tradition in Catholic ethics.[12]

Bioethics is the organization of ethical norms particularly among professionals of all kinds, from physicians to lawyers, in the North Atlantic civilization that is still recoiling from what the most highly educated people of Europe, who created the norms of university life for the nineteenth and twentieth century until 1933, did to fellow human beings, and especially what the men of medicine perpetrated, from 1933 to 1945. Over bioethics still swirl the fumes of camp laboratories, the cyanide spray of the gruesome bathhouses, the settling soot of the crematoria.

A second point, drawn from the history of our key word, is that some hold that the emerging crystalline structure of biomedical knowledge and skills is of such complex parameters, of such frightening innovation, as to be regarded by ethicists as different from any other sphere covered thus far by ethics. These ethicists would regard bioethics as a discipline apart. Others hold that the discipline of ethics is only being stretched to accommodate new times and technologies: an ethics of extrapolation and argument from analogy.

For some theological ethicists of the first type, "the soul" has been replaced by "the person" as the term that can best gain acceptance in the public domain; and the ethicist of the first or second type can vigorously and resourcefully defend the continuum which is the human being, a person from conception.[13] In any case, bioethicists, whether they regard their field as a branch of ethics or a discrete discipline, are desperately seeking to establish new definitions of human life.

III. Five Christian Approaches to Bioethics

Turning to a Christian theological approach to our themes, I now specify the five possible theological approaches that were distinguished at the already mentioned ecumenical and international consultation at Bossey in 1968. To catch them in a phrase or two, they would be: (1) man created in the image of God participates in the continuous process of co-creation and procreation, beholding in Jesus Christ what man in the image of God means, surely merciful, healing, illuminating; (2) natural law is common to all men; it is not the law of animate and inanimate creatures but only this law insofar as it is hominized; and we discern this law in our members, in our human nature, only as we observe it in time and space beyond regional and class-bound transcriptions of it; (3) all of human nature is fallen, and human life is broken and to some degree alienated from God and from other bearers of the same nature, whether we take literally or as profoundly mythical the biblical account of the fall in our *libido sentiendi, sciendi, dominandi*; (4) Jesus Christ came in humility and suffered on the cross to come again in judgment and definitive salvation, the healing of nations no less than of individuals; hence bioethics should be placed in an eschatological context; (5) the cosmic Christ of Ephesians, Philippians, and Colossians is the redeemer of all men, whether they know it or not, for because of him as the instrument of God's salvific purpose the whole of creation has been taken up in the divine Love which penetrates all nature and history. This is a theme prominent in the Greek Fathers, revived by Teilhard de Chardin, S.J., and fundamental in the documents of Vatican II.[14]

IV. Natural Law and the Updated Hippocratic Tradition as Basis of a Christian Bioethics

There are at least five reasons for choosing natural law as the basis for elaborating a bioethics from a Christian point of view insofar as that might at any point be distinct, in the modern world of medicine, from a purely humane and compassionate view. And, unlike the consultants near Geneva, I would go expressly beyond the Catholic-humanistic view to include in it, as did many ancients and moderns, the laws of the cosmos and hence of all living nature.

It is commonly objected by Protestants that natural law is a legacy of classical antiquity, incorporated into Catholic natural theology, and used as the basis of Catholic teaching in areas particularly of morals where it is desirable to appeal to a non-confessional consensus. However, despite the unequivocal views of Martin Luther against the natural law in matters of concern to faith, along with the somewhat greater openness to the possibility of a natural law in Calvinism, if less in John Calvin himself, eventually Lutheran and Reformed and Anglican thought alike came to legitimate for Protestantism the natural law.

Protestants became appreciatively aware that Cicero in his *Tusculan Disputations* (I) had observed that "the consent of all nations is the law of nature" and that Domitius Ulpian in his *Institutiones* (I) of ca. 220 A.D. had understood natural law as including all of nature: "The law which nature has taught to all living creatures . . . is common to man and beast."

The early rabbinical concept of Noachite laws that were expected to be known by non-Jews and heeded constituted a body of precepts comparable in many ways to classical natural law. Moreover, St. Paul was expressly a supporter of natural law. In his address on Mars Hill Paul recognized that the creative teleological principle in the cosmos was already known to peoples beyond the ken of the Hebrew prophets. He quoted the poet Aratus of Soli in Cilicia (d. ca. 340 B.C.), *Phaenomena, 5*: "Yet he [God] is not far from each one of us [whether Greek or Barbarian], for 'in him we live and move and have our being'; as even some of your poets have said" (Acts 17:28). And in his Epistle to the Romans, where we have his own direct words, the first chapter is an affirmation of natural law or Noachite law, especially in verses 19-32, which begin: "For what can be known about God is plain to them [Jew and Gentile, Greek and Barbarian]. Ever since the creation of the world his invisible nature, namely, his eternal power and deity, has been clearly perceived in the things that have been made." Thus Paul is an important sanction for our use of natural law in the double sense of the law of nations and the laws of non-hominized nature; and he even uses the distinction of natural and unnatural use (*physika chresis* in contrast to usage *para physin*) (v. 26).[15]

The major theological achievement of Elizabethan Anglicanism distinguished various kinds of law, including the law of nature: *The Laws of Ecclesiastical Polity* by Richard Hooker. Francis Bacon declared: "Nature cannot be commanded except by being obeyed." The founder of modern international law, the Dutch Remonstrant jurist, Hugo Grotius, in the macrobioethical realm of *De jure belli ac pacis* (I) in 1625, went so far as to declare: "The law of nature is so unalterable that it cannot be changed by God Himself."

Today we are aware, however, that in the submolecular realm and in the astrophysical realm alike a principle of randomness confronts us. In the macrobioethical realm we are baffled by how we can use or suppress a submolecular process that can cinderize large portions of the civilized world in an unimaginable holocaust.

In the microbioethical realm we face comparable vagaries as the specialists themselves, with their various agendas, are not always clear even to themselves. Frightening prospects as well as hopes repose in genetic mechanics, natural and induced mutations, and above all in human intervention into genetic, sexual, and psychic behavior. So much fundamental alteration of human nature, not to say animal nature, is now possible or within range of biomedical technology that Grotius's observation that "the law of nature is so unalterable that it cannot be changed by God Himself" must now be taken as utterly invalidated, not only in the macrobiological realm of the laws of nations but also in the microbiological realm of interpersonal relations involving biomedical intervention. *Or* it may be taken as a solemn warning out of our past.

Among the five reasons for preferring natural law in the Christian approach to bioethics, the *first* is that in no other realm of ethics could revealed religion of any kind, Jewish or Christian, be of sufficient specificity to extrapolate from it principles and then those middle axioms by which we enter the intricate maze of the new decision-making demanded by microbioethics. *Secondly,* in no realm of ethics are we so close to the interface of the operation of the natural laws governing not only life but the physics and chemistry of the created order. We are at the workbench of the Creator and, with both awe and legitimate curiosity, we discern how much more wondrous is creation than ever the Psalmist could have known, looking at the night sky or counting the sands of the seashore for the number. And this created order is the same for the Marxist as for the Methodist, for the Sunnite biologist in Cairo University and the Sikh physicist from the Punjab engaged in experiments in New Delhi. *Thirdly,* any ethical system can become so involved in its own normative system that it loses contact with the biophysical reality in which it is supposed to be relevant for decision-making. Aristotle was the best biologist of his day; but the ethical system of Thomas Aquinas based on that biology, and specifically on that fetology, makes many of the specific precepts of the Angelic Doctor unacceptably irrelevant because, as ethicist of his age, he depended on the biology and fetology of Aristotle.

For us who are microbiologists and for us who are microbio-ethicists, for the last score of years the most universal natural law, a principle unifying all life from the amoeba to man, is the genetic code in which the DNA through the macromolecular messenger RNA signals the selection of the twenty amino acids to make the proteins in the varied patterns of the diversified species and individuals, imparting to them their capacity for replication of the species and sufficiently varied to allow for mutation and hence for evolving diversification of life.[16]

Fourthly, in the microbioethical field, perhaps less so in the macrobioethical realm, professionals on the biomedical side see the same things and can anticipate the same developments whether they are Jews, agnostics, Catholics, or visiting medical scholars from religious cultures entirely different from the ever more pluralistic civilization of the North Atlantic community and its provinces around the globe. Indeed, it is becoming

increasingly invalid to speak of even this as a distinct community, with respect to medical research. Ultimately in bioethics
we are dealing with the actual or at least potential concerns of
advanced and developing societies alike.

The *fifth* advantage of natural law is that without the use of
expressly Judeo-Christian terminology, we who are Jews or
Christians or indeed Muslims are enabled, within the inherited
resources of natural law as supposedly common to all human
nature and combined at the microbioethical level with growing
knowledge about the physical, chemical, and biological laws, to
engage in common research without obtruding our belief in
God as Creator and of ourselves in some sense created in his
image, and without raising the issue of confessional or ideo-
logical affiliation or the lack thereof, and yet be in a position to
discuss the issues, as indeed in this seminar, as Christians.

If the WCC Consultation of 1968, which may have been the
seedbed in which the new word "bioethics" sprouted, had
distinguished five theological approaches discussed but largely
inoperative, I have taken one of those options, natural law, as
the basis of what I wish to say further. What Christianity does
for us primarily, insofar as we are in touch with scripture and
tradition as normative, is to make us as medical or legal
practitioners truthful, fair, and compassionate. I also think that
healing in the New Testament accounts of Jesus' ministry and
that of his followers have been too long regarded as wholly
apostolic gifts that disappeared with the last eyewitnesses of
Jesus' decisive witness on the Cross. At long last, spiritual
healing has reentered the churches of mainstream Protestantism and Catholicism and miracles still abound in the name of
the Lord.

In elaborating the middle axioms for bioethics within the
context of natural law, one can see a time when not only the
ancient distinctions of Greek and Barbarian, Jew and Gentile,
woman and man, fetus and genius, human beings and animals,
will have lost their sharpness in an increasing prevalence in us of
the merciful over the malevolent, of the compassionate over the
cruel streak in us, until at length the whole of creation, groaning

together no more in travail, will rejoice in the adoption of the sons and daughters of Eve and Adam; and we shall behold the redemption not only of our souls but also of our bodies (cf. Rom. 8:22f), for we are indeed already one body, the embodiment as the human race of the grand design of that ultimate Father and the mysterious Matrix of the cosmos, in whom, we make bold to say again with St. Paul, we live and move and have our being.

To be sure, ancient medicine was not wholly a caring profession. Doctors did not always take cases they could not cure. Compassion or caring was not the outstanding trait of the ancient physician.[17] And it would appear to be in Francis Bacon (d. 1626) that we have evidence of a concern to prolong life, almost against the Hippocratic oath, with a view to ascertaining the possible causes of so-called incurable diseases in order to help others in like circumstances. In the meantime, Bacon urged the caring doctor to befriend and comfort by his presence, even if he could not help, in order to observe the suffering and dying patient, aiding him in a "natural [or "outward"] euthanasia," as well as promoting that "spiritual euthanasia" made possible by "the preparation of the soul" in the presence of a praying minister or a confessor priest.[18]

V. Seven Axioms for Bioethics Growing Out of Natural Law and the Hippocratic Tradition

At this point it is appropriate to introduce several axioms that would appear to derive from an updated natural law with special reference to bioethics, although insofar as the axioms derive from the Hippocratic school, we must acknowledge that the religio-philosophical content thereof was esoteric—atypical of medical guilds of the Graeco-Roman world—and quite probably Pythagorean. In any case, the Pythagorians alone among ancient philosophical schools unequivocally opposed suicide and abortion.[19] But even if the Hippocratic tradition arose within a particular philosophical school concerning the soul (transmigration) and the body, its more than two millenia of influence in medical ethics imparts to the corpus an imposing status.

One of the seven axioms—wholly of my own selection and ordering—is already part of the Hippocratic corpus and may be said to constitute a middle axiom of bioethics based upon natural law already firmly embedded in medical ethics in the Hippocratic oath, in two places: namely, to act "never with a view to injury" and to abstain "from all intentional . . . harm," and in the *Epidemics* ". . . at least, . . . to do no harm."[20]

A *second* axiom, twice asseverated in the Hippocratic oath is "I shall act in my patient's interest," and "No house shall I enter, but in the interests of my patients."

A *third* axiom from the Hippocratic corpus, from *On the Art of Medicine* ("art" being Greek *techne,* which gives us our word "technology"), where the assignments of medicine or of the physician are enumerated, is the refusal "to treat those who are overmastered by their diseases" in the realization "that in such cases medicine is powerless."[21] This third axiom is complicated for us by the fact that the ancient mentor of physicians could not foresee a time when, as we approach the 2450th anniversary of his birth, physicians, still swearing to a modified form of his oath, would have to face the dilemma of refusal to prolong life or otherwise alter another person when their medical art—now definitely also a technology—can, even against "the best interest of the patient," save him because in many "such cases medicine is [in fact, no longer] powerless." While we all agree that a physician of such antiquity cannot have the decisive word about what the men of biomedicine face, if we acknowledge the weight of the Hippocratic tradition in medical ethics, we must grant that the weight of the axiom is to withhold heroic measures to prolong or fundamentally to alter life afflicted by several diseases consumptive and agonizing, even if the art of modern medicine has the technology to intervene and this because of the second axiom which constrains the physician to "act in [the] patient's interest."[22]

The idea that the physician has a responsibility to prolong life is not classical. We have already observed that it can be traced to

Francis Bacon and his generation and that it was linked in his mind with biomedical research. Highly contrived means of prolonging life when there is not expectation of recovery is also against religious traditions, Christian and Jewish among them with related eschatologies. For Christians there was traditionally also the idea that terminal suffering was an aspect of everyman's *imitatio Christi* (*crucifixio*).

The *fourth* axiom is close to the third but in partial contradiction to it. The fourth axiom is not at the interface of the painful death of a patient and the powerlessness of medicine; it is not even at the border of the patient's best interest and the doctor's power. It is rather *in* the border zone between the patient's plight and the physician's duty in his ever expanding power to effect alterations in another human being that so far exceed what now seems natural and congruous that they seem to imperil what is human and humane. The fourth axiom relates to the responsibility of the physician to himself and his profession—and hence to other patients within range of the doctor's concern and also future patients and possible cures for them—to prolong life for the study of morbidity, so long as no harm is done to the patient immediately under the doctor's care. The governing word in the emergent axiom involves the patient's "bearing," an intentionally comprehensive and elastic term and necessarily linked with a sense of proportionality in the physician.

The concept of *bearing*, linked with others, interposes itself at the point where the dignity of the patient and his desires are accommodated to the mandate of medicine to advance. Humane physicians and ethicists have long sought to define the safeguards of the dignity of the patient, the rights of the patient, the personhood of the patient, his wholeness as the definition of his health, and more abstractly his humanhood.

The last term, humanhood, is that of a clerical ethicist who pioneered in modern medical ethics, finally renounced his ordination and his Christianity, and proceeded, as a humane secular humanist, to work out an integrated medical ethics from which many, if not most, religious and many other ethicists in the same field turn away: Joseph Fletcher.[23]

In groping to formulate an axiom in cases of multiple affliction, judged by Hippocrates to be beyond the power of medicine but now within its power, the attempts to define life, human life, humanhood, personhood, are on the right track; but the clarification of the appropriate axiom and the reaching of a consensus as to where the physician and biomedical researcher should rest his case still lie ahead for specialists of all kinds.

In defining a human being for the purpose of medical ethics we once spoke in terms of body and soul; now we speak in terms of body and brain waves.[24] In several millennia of the medical effort to locate somatically the essence of the human being and of human life, we moved from the soul and breath (in the case of the biblical Jews and the Stoics), through the blood (in the case of the biblical Jews), the "bowels" (meaning such organs as the heart and the womb, where some of our deepest feelings are experienced), and now to the brain waves. The report of 1968 of the Ad Hoc Committee of the Harvard Medical School to Examine the Definition of Brain Death[25] marked a watershed in medical ethics in making irreversible coma the crucial datum in determining death, which goes on in different parts of a dying person at different rates, in the hair last of all. Since even that definition excludes that part of the brain which controls the automatic nervous system or which can be stimulated to do so, and since cephalic transplants have already been successfully executed with monkeys, we should be on guard lest further research and even drastic psychosurgery reveal that whole sections of the brain and the brain itself are dispensable and we are left with nothing indispensably, personally human. Though we are basing our thought on natural law and not revelation, Christians know well that the Apostles' Creed and its conciliar successors uphold faith in "the resurrection of the body"; and they should, therefore, remind themselves that Christians, unlike the aberrant Gnostics, took seriously the incarnation of the eternally begotten Son of God and, serious about Christ's flesh and the relics of saints, were not Docetists.

The axiom we still seek to define personhood in modern

terms must include body, breath, bowels, brain, and *bearing*. This last term, already anticipated, may seem to be dictated by so adventitious a consideration as alliteration. But I have sought a word more inclusive than volition, one which also involves human relationship and thus allows for another person to act for a comatose or senile person by previously expressed intention on the part of the afflicted or *ex officio* by reason of relationship to the person so incapacitated. For a place in natural law it is not necessary that it have scriptural sanction; but the word in its verbal form is used in 1 Corinthians 13:7 and 15:49 in decisive ways; and there are parallels to this habitual bearing (*phoreo*) in classical Greeks. (In scholastic Latin, part of the meaning of *bearing* is derived from *habeo: habitus.*)

The root of "bearing" also gives us "birth." Bearing is a strangely comprehensive word, and almost all its specialized meanings can be used by extension of human beings. To be sure, all mammals are born; but only human beings among them, having borne the burdens of life with a bearing distinctive of their personalities and who come to understand the bearing of events, that is their meaning, may in the end perhaps begin to lose their bearings, and these human beings have a bearing even in senility that must be respected. Moreover, the same word suggests the capacity to bear suffering as meaningful. Bioethics must take seriously the totality of the human being, not life alone, whether defined as soul, breath, or brain waves, but that kind of life that has bearing, whether potentially or retrospectively, a neurosomatic unity in successive stages of development and decline or sudden destruction from accident or disease. This is not to rule out the new brain-wave definition of death, but to insist that it be kept under continuous review. And as to the norms that might now govern practice with respect to the "passive" termination of life of gravely defective neonates and the incurable and comotose aged, I would agree with the positions represented in the articles of Harold Brown and Peter Riga. The fourth axiom, involving the bearing of the patient and the bearing of what the doctor does in respect to him, is an axiom in which the mandate of medicine to advance its cures is acknowledged. And bearing also relates to macrobioethics.

A *fifth* axiom relates to unborn human life, which also has its context, its voluntary or involuntary origin—that is from the point of view of the bearing mother—and a succession of fetal phases that, while largely but not wholly immune to the immediate and the larger social environment of the mother, has its own bearing, as it were, its own genetic code, its own inherent laws of fetological maturation. In the Hippocratic oath the caveat against an "abortifacient tampon" (*pesson phthorion*), while it stood apart from medical and general practice in the ancient world and while even in Hippocrates the concern was as much to "keep pure and holy both" the life (*bios*) of the physician and his "art" (*techne*), makes it clear that Hippocrates and his school understood fetal life itself to be "pure and holy" and not to be tampered with. In this aversion to abortion we know that Hippocrates and his school stood apart from other physicians, and this possibly explains also his unwillingness to make use of the knife, in other words, to act the surgeon. In historical forthrightness it must be acknowledged, therefore, that the Hippocratic tradition about the inviolability of the fetus had philosophical, and therefore also religious, presuppositions as to the origin of the soul, which was held to antedate indeed the beginning of fetal life, while modern medicine and biology, through no fault of either discipline, are unable to isolate this entity. But the Hippocratic axiom that came to be generally accepted by the society that created modern medicine cannot be dispensed with simply because that ancient psychology, in the most precise sense of that word, cannot be held by modern physicians and indeed is in the Pythagorean form regarded as a heresy by Christians—that is, the preexistence of souls. At the same time, we today know more wondrous things about genetics and fetology than ever Aristotle or Hippocrates could have envisaged as possible, such that our responsibility for not tampering with human life on its way in the womb seems even clearer now than when it was believed by Aristotle to be successively informed by a vegetative, then an animal, then a rational soul. Such a succession of infused or coinheriting souls (earlier in male chauvinist antiquity, of course, for embryonic boys than girls!) was also held to advance without any maternal counterpart of the male seed: only Galen would later make the correct surmise. Thus in spite of so much better knowledge of what early fetal life is than the ancients, the Hippocratic oath still provides us with an axiom, made more explicit in the Geneva Declaration of 1948: "I will maintain the utmost respect for human life from the time of conception."

Nevertheless, the pro-life extremists must not be allowed to construe abortifacient contraception in the Fallopian tube or before implantation of the embryo along with its potential placental cells in the wall of the uterus as "murder," any more than a judge confuses various degrees of manslaughter and various degrees of murder. The Hippocratic oath itself distinguished between the mercy killing of a patient by poison, and abortion.

The fifth axiom is that human life begins from the moment that the sperm and ovum join to form the diploid generation: the single-cell zygote. But (1) the aboriginal union which takes place in the Fallopian tube can be fatal for the mother and *conceptus* if the zygote/embryo does not descend to the uterus or becomes ectopically implanted elsewhere; (2) some of the same cells that constitute that embryo of 32 or 64 undifferentiated cells at implacement in the uterus specialize to form the placenta, a complicated temporary organ that secures nutrition while preventing mammalian mothers from ejecting the implanted fetus as a "foreign" body (not wholly compatible with her body), and ejected eventually as the afterbirth; (3) the clustering of zygote cells can develop as a set of identical twins or triplets; and finally (4) more than half of mammalian *conceptus* are naturally aborted, including those of women in a substantial percentage of cases (in one French study only 16 percent not aborted) because of defects as serious as being triploid rather than diploid.

We may therefore refrain from speaking of the zygote and even the cluster of embryonic cells while still in the Fallopian tube as *a* person. I say this as myself an opponent of abortion from the time when, as a boy, I first learned what the word meant. But bioethics and biomedical practice in the United States cannot be placed on a sounder *bearing* than is now possible with the Supreme Court ruling of 22 January 1973 unless the opponents of the abortion of sentient children (surely the most grievous form of abortion) are willing to make clear distinctions among contraception, natural and artificial; conception of the zygote in the Fallopian tube; implantation of the multi-celled but undifferentiated embryo in the uterus; abortion of intrauterine life or lives; and infanticide of the gravely defective neonates, active or passive. Hence willing, in the public domain, despite personal repugnance or theological scruple, to allow room for a political convergence or coalition in a pluralistic society that will succeed in inhibiting abortion of the *implanted fetus,* with all biologists we can affirm the zygote and the cell-cluster in the Fallopian tube as human being, as human life, but not, for the four reasons given above, as *a* human being, as *a person.* This argument for an embryonic distinction that would, of course, legitimate contraceptively intended abortifacients within the Fallopian tube is not, of course, an argument from natural law but from at least some valid distinction between human life in the tube and the human person or persons in the womb and thus possibly enable all of anti-abortionist sentiment to garner the votes for a Federal amendment or statute that will ideally end almost all surgical abortions.

It is difficult to trace the phrase "sanctity of [human] life." In the church there are saints who are eventually canonized, the blessed, and the large company of humanity *simul lapsa et redempta.* In any case some distinction between the *locus et characta embryonis* and the *locus fetus qua personae* is analagous to distinctions in degrees of manslaughter and in murder, which are partly defined at law by the intent of the perpetrator.

A *sixth* axiom comes, not from ancient oaths and medical practice, but from modern experience, although it can make out for itself a fairly venerable pedigree. Bioethics, in the sense of microbioethics brought into focus by biomedical research and practices, cannot be dealt with myopically or monocularly as a wholly enclosed province of general ethics. Microbioethics must be carried on bifocally, with an awareness for macrobioethics or environmental ethics. The oncologist who coined the term "bioethics," Dr. Van Rensselaer Potter, was much concerned not only with the human, social, and natural environment in which carcenogenic toxins created the disease of his specialty but also for the creation of a terminology for a discipline that "might build a 'bridge to the future' by building the discipline of Bioethics as bridge between the two cultures" of the natural sciences and the humanities.

Bioethics commonly tends to be exclusively tied to the laboratory, the operating room, and the special nursery. But there is the macrobioethics of Love Canal, of Three Mile Island, the sheep ranges of the atomic test sites of Utah and Nevada, and the Agent Orange defoliated jungles of Vietnam, since a humanly polluted unnatural environment of perduring toxins that cause birth defects in sperm and ovum, no less than *in utero*, must be considered as reprehensible and morally irresponsible in comparison with the at least benign intent of the most acceptable form of *in vitro* fertilization.

Nor may the microbioethicist pursue his refined arguments in isolation from the enormous problems of the macrobioethicist. We are all shocked by the warning (1982) of the Secretary General of the United Nations from Peru, Perez de Cuellar, that 40,000 children die in the world *each day* because of imbalance in the distribution of the resources of the planet.

Thus my sixth axiom is that microbioethics must be pursued with an awareness of macrobioethics and so far as possible the two emphases must be kept in touch with each other. I prefer this formulation of the axiom rather than the more common cost-effectiveness formula, which is too closely linked to microbioethics and American medical facilities and the American economy. In microbioethics we do not deal often with the concerns of doctors in public health, of specialists in world health organizations under various auspices. But the sixth axiom involves global proportionality as well as local proportionality with respect to means and ends.

In natural law, Grotius, thinking of it primarily as the law of nations (*jus gentium*), in the context of his epoch-making treatise on peace and war, discussed the doctrine of the just war, as transmitted from classical antiquity by Augustine and Aquinas, the proportionality of appropriate means to legitimate military goals. (The deliberations of the American Catholic Bishops Conference of 15 November 1982 and their debated pastoral letter on nuclear deterrence drew upon this just-war tradition.) In a sense in the practice of medicine, especially against ever new strains of self-immunized bacteria and viruses through genetic mutation, in resisting antibiotics and in the practice of public health there is a kind of waging of war, whether it be the malady of a single patient, or an epidemic, or a new classification of disease. And in the assault vast sums are expended and even international strategies are mounted.

In the waging of the wars of medicine, proportionality must be factored into any decision as to the use of medical facilities and sheer time of professionals. Indeed, proportionality could be extrapolated from the Geneva oath of 1948 (above at n. 9), which does not "permit considerations of nationality . . . or social standing" or the possession of private means to deflect the medical profession from any measure it can privately or publicly devise in order to keep access to medical skills and technology open to all. Heed to *bearing* keeps in view the legitimate claims of the patient to humane care from the doctor to whom he is entrusted, especially in problematic and medically noteworthy cases; heed to proportionality inhibits the doctor from both excessive preoccupation with hopeless cases and excessive means in solving any class of medical problems. While "excessive" will vary in scope in hospitals and laboratories in different parts of the world and no doubt in the unfolding of medical proficiency, still natural law, on the analogy of the just-war theory, invokes restraint.

This leads to the *seventh* axiom. It relates to animals. The brains of chimpanzees and their sensibility to pain comes close to that of any human fetus and even of a child at its earlier stage of development. A dog sitting in the front seat of a car by his master, despite a few movements on the part of the driver, feels that the two are doing approximately the same thing: riding. The dog is visibly moved by his or her sense of the oneness in love and companionableness and even honorable equality in the front seat. In the limited brain of the dog, but in the emotionally rather highly hominized heart in trust and love, he or she and the master or mistress are gazing out upon the passing scenery in blissful bonds of oneness. In the Alexandrian medical theatre of classical antiquity prisoners were vivisected. The Emperor Frederick II (d. 1250) of the Holy Roman Empire in this tradition looked at close range upon the vivisection of a serf in what was the beginnings of the medical faculty of the University of Naples. What I have to say about vivisection is not obscurantist. It is in line with the best intentions of most men and women of medicine and the laboratory practices of biomedics. But it needs to be said that bioethics concerns the ethics of life and that while we understand thereby human life, the New Biology links us so closely with the higher and even the lowest forms of life that for the sake of the unborn child, for the sake of the senile insane parent, for the sake of the mangled body taken from the highway crash into the emergency ward, we must give thought to all suffering and even, if on a lower level, to the dignity of life below that which is human. We instinctively felt that it is close to murder when a male gorilla, slowly hominized by trust in and communication with the woman anthropologist in Rwanda, was slain in the night by local people and beheaded and prepared for cooking.

All creatures belong to the Great Chain of Being in time and ecological interdependence, and in the case of domestic animals, by the extension of the covenant—a legacy of Judaism. Albert Schweitzer, the theologian, as a medical student destined to become a physician dissected human cadavers and perhaps engaged in the vivisection of animals. His great phrase "reverence for life" came to him when at dusk he saw hippopotamuses rise from the river near his hospital in the jungle and forage on the shores of a tributary of the Congo near Lambarene. His term expressly included thus all forms of life.

It represents an advance in this area that Pope John Paul II in several communications and most recently in his address before his own Pontifical Academy of Science, 23 October 1982, "On Biological Experimentation," wherein he declared: "It is certain that animals are at the service of man and can hence be the object of experimentation. Nevertheless, they must be treated *as creatures of God* which are destined to serve man's good, but not to be abused by him. Hence the diminution of experimentation on animals, which has progressively been made ever less necessary, corresponds to the well-being of all creation."[26]

The seventh and final axiom is, then, that to the degree that we in biomedical thought and practice comprehend subhuman and sentient life within the covenant of our human mercy, reckoning immediate human benefit in the context of the sensibilities of not only the human experimenter but also of custodians and all others who are exposed to the plaintive cries of all beings used for a higher order of life, that higher order of life itself will be less likely to be turned into mere objects; and people, whether doctors, patients, or attendants and technicians, will themselves be more generally compassionate.

VI. The Sacred Condominium as an Ethical Model of Decision-Making Authorities Particularly in Microbioethics

With some seven middle axioms drawn from the Hippocratic tradition and natural law, with others no doubt already identified and other axioms yet to be identified and characterized, we recognize as particularly problematic in microbioethics the rapid advances over a vast surface that seems to be churning and pulling us into itself like a swamp of mingled quicksand and quicksilver. For conscientious doctors and biomedical researchers there is a need for something like at once a court and a forum. The Presidential Commission on Medical Ethics, set up by Jimmy Carter and reporting on 17 November 1982, recognizes the need to monitor and coordinate the many local review boards.

In reaching justice in the more public domain there is the law; common, statutory, and regulatory, with a body of precedents to extrapolate from; there is the grand distinction between civil and criminal cases; there is the court itself with its judiciary, jury, and lawyers public and private; and finally there are the various penalties, mandatory and discretionary, retributive and rehabilatory. Even if there comes to pass a federal commission, as recently recommended, there is still need of an institution called a medical court, or a medical forum/tribunal. There are various kinds of consultations, of specialists with each other, of the doctors with the patients and next of kin. There can perhaps be no medical court in the full juridical sense, but there can be its counterpart in a consensual procedure.

Within the biomedical and bioethical decision-making process there could be a chamber of deliberation, wherein there would not be a counterpart of a judge or a bench of justices. But there could be an analogous institutionalization of medical and biomedical procedure that would have participants or, as it were, functionaries, whose relative authority would shift by consensus in changing situations. I have elsewhere defined my concept of *the sacred condominium*.[27] The term may not be felicitous, for more than one reason, besides suggesting independently owned apartments in large buildings (popularly: condos).

The legal concept of the condominium and the term comes from public law and etymologically implies *co-sovereignty* and co-rule *in changing degrees of authority* depending upon the circumstances. The *sacred* condominium has possibilities as a model for bioethical decision-making and in helping to further define the roles of various participants in inchoate deliberative conferences that already go on.

In sixteenth-century Europe and thereafter, particularly in the Holy Roman Empire, there were many instances of joint rule by, for example, the King of Denmark and the Duke of Holstein over that duchy. This was a condominium *ex officiis*, that is, the King and the duke had come over a period of more than one generation to agree on whose ministers of state should exercise rule in the same territory. In other cases two brothers or cousins might rule over the same territory in alternate years, taxing and administering lands dynastically inherited. In a few instances, with a change of rule, came a change of religion, the cathedral, for example, being alternatively Catholic and Lutheran.[28] The word is not used in modern governmental or constitutional theory, but in any federated state where the superior sovereignty exercises co-sovereignty over the same population within a constituent unit of that larger political whole, we have, in effect, a political condominium: in America, in constitutional and legal parlance, "concurrent jurisdiction." But the condominium is different from concurrency. The value for us of reviving for adaptation the late feudal and early modern condominium is that, as it once functioned, the subjects of the lords were not involved; and only a handful of ministers of state and other specialized functionaries were taken up with mutual decision-making. A toll bridge erected by one lord during his rule had implications for the other. Moreover, depending on the situation the two or several lords or their plenipotentiaries had differently weighted judgments. Thus the condominial court is not like a court where the judge presides and gives orders and instructs jury and lawyers, the defendant, and witnesses. Furthermore, when in reviving the old term we add the adjective "sacred," we have a dynamic concept, model, and even the makings of a procedure for dealing with problems of all those directly involved in matters of life and death, health and wholeness, compassion and faithfulness to the solemn trust of life.

The sacred condominium of life is involved in bioethical and sometimes bioforensic decisions in the intracacies of a complex realm which constitutional and statutory and regulatory law can perhaps never penetrate with adequate precision or at least keep up with. In the sacred condominium there is a natural assignment of relative and shifting authority. In the case of a patient in full or sufficient control of his own mind and intention, *he* or *she* has the most authority within the sacred condominium except that he is constrained by law and custom from suicide; and any person in our society has the right to interpose himself to prevent this. In the case of the patient unable to speak for himself, the insane, the senile, the handicapped child, there would be designated, disinterested advocates *ex officiis* in the condominial proceedings (on which see further below).

With respect to the fetus, up until the gratuitously expanded scope of the decision of the Supreme Court of 22 January 1973, society rightly held that it had a concern in the life of the womb if the mother or the parents renounced their protective role as co-sovereigns with society in the protection of this new life. It was, in fact, in the atmosphere of American thought on abortion before the sweeping away of almost all restraints by the Supreme Court that I first developed the idea of the sacred condominium and at a time when I myself thought that the Court could find the fetus to be a full person before the law, as earlier two amendments to the Constitution so declared the antebellum slave. But so long as the Court remains unaltered by amendment or otherwise, the concept or model of the sacred condominium still has utility in the matter of abortion and abortion counseling, for it has been my view from the start that the parents or the mother and the natural father, if he wishes to be involved, are co-sovereign with society in the protection of life.

And until such a time as we have been able to change the law, the fetus should still have an advocate in the sacred condominium; and, as regards fetal research, unless it is expressly in the interest of the developing child, the mother who has chosen abortion has also relinquished her co-sovereignty over it; and her experimental doctor may not usurp it! The still residual concern of society for what we *all* know is human life insists the medical profession, grounded in its fundamental oath and safeguarded by statute if necessary, restrain itself *from all fetal research* that is not in the interest of any given fetal person.

The concept and model of the sacred condominium has

applicability to any area of bioethical and biomedical forensic concern.

In the deliberations of the sacred condominial forum/ tribunal there could be as many as three bioethical counterparts of the specialist in forensic medicine and the medical coroner in possibly criminal cases, namely, a doctor whose career is wholly devoted to the review of medical cases and experimental projects and a lawyer whose career is wholly devoted to the public interest in hard medical cases and biomedical projects. It is possible that to these two specialists, the forensic physician and the medical lawyer, there should be added to the panel the religiously trained bioethicist.

In the sacred condominial forum/tribunal the middle axioms of natural law would guide the deliberations by extrapolation and analogy. Basic would be whether a proposed medical intervention be construed in some sense as corrective and compensatory, and thus to some extent natural rather than inventive and even in the end subversive of human nature and the human person, lest manipulation go too far as skills and techniques turn patients into projects.[29]

Thus far I have left out the ordinary physicians and biomedical researchers at the frontiers of speculation, research, and hazardous practice. It is because from the start I have been building the argument for their right to semi-autonomy in this field, for their due status as professionals within the sacred condominium. We have seen that the contemporary concern for guidelines in bioethics and biomedical research was occasioned by the infamous taint of Naziism infecting the medical profession, and we saw the first post-war Declaration, that of Geneva of 1948, clearly modify the Hippocratic oath in language that would never have been needed had it not been for the war crimes of the profession. But the medical profession did not escape the Nazi taint any the more impregnated with ideology than the other professions. The Nazi governor of truncated Poland was the president of the German Academy of Jurists. Few priests and ministers were heroic in the face of the Nazi juggernaut. Thus I think it is possible that doctors themselves around the world and ethicists concerned with issues in the biomedical field have too long been overanxious that if doctors were left alone, they might become the physiological engineers of an Orwellian society. The other historical impetus in the emergence of bioethics is, in fact, the conscience of physicians and biomedical researchers themselves reaching out for counsel in the increasingly difficult realms into which their very expertise has driven them.

The Hippocratic oath presupposes a guild or society of "all who have taken the physician's oath, . . . holding such things [professional lore and usage] to be holy secrets." In the more open language of the Geneva Declaration, modeled on the oath, there survives the brotherhood of professionals who pledge to keep the secrets, in this case, of their patients entrusted to them. But, alas, this association has in some countries become so nearly a union and a business operation and even a lobby, concerned with self-protection, that non-doctors seldom realize the extent to which within that professional carapace there still survives among almost all physicians the ancient sense of a highly responsible and taxing confraternity of medical minis- trants. It would be the hope of many that local and regional and national associations of the men and women of medicine could clarify, for themselves and then for the public, these two aspects of the ancient guild in its modern form and then help restore, for the good of society and their own sense of high calling, the relative autonomy of their collegial guild and thus enhance or restore the sense of confidence of patients in their doctors and free the doctors from the fear of frivolous litigious reprisals. The submission of difficult cases by physicians to the sacred condominial court/tribunal should become recognized as safe- guarding their own professional authority.

As a university professor I cannot imagine working under regulations imposed from without. Indeed, a professional man of the so-called free professions, the traditional learned professions—theology, law, and medicine—was characterized by being self-monitoring. All three of them deal with the ultimates of life and death, but the doctor, far more than even the lawyer, lives in the environment of emerging and terminating life and the suffering in between. It is understandable, therefore, that his free profession and his professional association should be much more complex and subject to much more external scrutiny than the other two. But I feel very strongly that the litigious character of American society has permitted us to go altogether too far in subjecting physicians and surgeons to malpractice suits in the area of bioethical concern and to besmirch conscientious treatment and becloud licit research with fear on the part of doctors and researchers.

It is precisely here the institutionalization of the sacred condominium would have an additional benefit. Once a medical association has distinguished its wholly union- or business-like functions and refined the important residual collegial responsibilities that are truly professional in the earlier sense of ministrant and humane, then duly designated or elected members of the association could elaborate further what constitutes the collegial fraternity committed to "maintain by all means . . . the honor and noble traditions of the medical profession" lest anything be done under the auspices of the profession "contrary to the laws of humanity," that is, to natural law, to paraphrase and quote the Declaration of Geneva of 1948.

If in difficult cases the approved records and minutes of the institutionalized sacred condominial deliberations show that a physician or surgeon or biomedical experimenter has submitted his or her problem to the appropriate members of the condominial deliberative forum, then it is my argument that such persons should not be liable to suits against them because of a failure or miscarriage of medicine and research in these difficult new fields. This is not to rule out malpractice suits in ordinary cases, but in the complex field exposed to the scrutiny of biomedical researchers and bioethicists alike, practitioners, as distinguished from theorists, should not incur greater risk so long as the problem area was dealt with deliberatively in the kind of medical forum, quite different from the medical theatre, of which the feudal condominium is the model. In medicine and surgery and biomedical research it is not a matter of carbon paper but human tissue, not books but human bodies, not opinions but taxing operations. And the inherent compassion of the men of medicine should not be congealed by the fear of punitive and retaliatory litigation but rather by their own collegial fear of trespassing inadvertently beyond "the holy secrets" of their plighted oath, beyond the seven or so middle axioms of that oath and natural law, or beyond statutory law.

Some of us might have once been in "the condominial territory," as it were. And others of us may in senility or agony enter that domain. Unlike the defendant in a legal court, the patient, whether fetus or voluntary experimentee, or the terminally senile insane in pain, or a fully sovereign patient facing a hemicorporectomy or some other grossly mutilating operation, or the mentally ill, has in the communal court and forum the prevailing authority, directly or through a designated or previously chosen deputy or advocate within the deliberations of the whole. Often a bioethicist, religiously motivated, should participate as *advocatus* in the condominial deliberations, ideally with a mastery of both micro- and macrobioethical ethics, but guided also by any known confessional variants of the basic middle axioms as they might apply in the case of a matured patient no longer *compos mentis*. In the intricate variety of problems that would be deliberated in the condominial fora, mercy and compassion, not eugenic considerations, could be interposed to inhibit medical and medico-technical power from effecting consequences incongruous with, even repellently contrary to, the proper goal of all medicine: the health and wholeness of a patient as person insofar as the means and ends are consonant with "the patient's best interest." Increasingly, the condominial forum would define and refine "substitutive judgment" in the interest of preventing its becoming a euphemism for the best interest of the patient's family, doctor, or other persons and interests.

So long as there are some two thousand genetically based diseases like sickle-cell anemia, genetic engineering will probably in all cases be considered in the deliberations as benign and consonant with the natural law principle of *correction* and *compensation*. By the same token, it would appear likely that the identification of genetic clusters connected with behavioral traits and their alteration, pharmaceutical alteration of personality without the patient's consent, genetically monitored alteration of behavior through the cooperation of sociobiology and genetic engineering, would all be borderline cases. Surely the alteration of the sperm and ova, the introduction of human genetic material into apes for the purpose of enabling the experimenter to work with "subhuman hybrids," possibly for organ transplants, some excesses in organ transplanting, blueprinting personality by various contrived means, would all be ruled out forever by the deliberations of the sacred condominium.

The feudal territorial condominia were exceptional and interspersed among standard sovereignties. I envisage only a few medical condominial domains, most of them only on the margins of ordinary medical practice and biomedical research. But over the generations deliberations within these fora would accumulate precedents consonant with natural law and statutory law and made accessible in published reference form for consultation, with monitoring and coordination of the local condominial fora by a federal commission. "Landmark" decisions would be reached in certain hospital courts that would have immediate implications for procedures in other hospitals and laboratories, as is the case of state-court findings on the general practice of American law. The consensual precedents of the new kind of hospital or laboratory review board—new in being a condominium involving more persons than is now the case—would acquire status in the medical and the biomedical profession, which urgently needs guidelines on frontiers opened up over which statutory law can in many cases no longer legislate knowledgeably about, except for the enabling law needed by the hospital or laboratory to legitimate a condominial tribunal.

The sacred condominial fora of hospitals could then become specialized courts with a distinctive place in jurisprudence, as courts of equity, courts martial, juvenile courts, academic disciplinary sittings, and the other specialized courts of society.

VII. Conclusion

In addressing the problem of bioethics I am appealing in conclusion to the professional sense in doctors and their biomedical allies to continue to promote an ethical sensibility, in co-responsibility, as the primary legitimation of their licit claim to a degree of limited sovereignty within the sacred condominium.

As a non-medic I would argue that there is in each profession, now broadly conceived, whether that of the firefighter, the soldier, the journalist, the undertaker, the superintendent of cemeteries, the psychiatrist, the therapist of the wards of the senile insane, the custodians of the special nurseries, the nurse, the military chaplain, the supervisor of laboratories engaged in animal experimentation, the social worker, the lawyer, even that of the biblical scholar and theologian, the need, as for physicians, surgeons, and biomedical researchers, for privacy and mutual trust in order to talk freely among themselves and even make some decisions in view of their specialized problems, in the light of their illumined consciences and for the common good.

Every professional group has to be able to deliberate in the atmosphere of mutual confidence engendered when professionals of common concerns share freely with each other the problems they confront. There are difficult, sometimes repellent, sometimes depressing, sometimes hazardous, and sometimes almost so unbearably intricate aspects of many professions that it is better if the general public can be spared some of the details but never to the extent that any profession becomes a law unto itself. At the core of perhaps two-thirds of the professions broadly defined there is a dark area of procedure and enigmatic meaning that only the specialists can grapple with; and we who are not specialists cannot all take on these heavy burdens. Yet, neither can we leave them solely with the specialists and especially is this true in micro- and macrobiology under the ballooning canopy of bioethics. Since bioethics deals with human life, all human beings have a stake in the principles fashioned and elaborated. The upshot of what may appear to be a slight relativism or indecisiveness on my part is in fact decisive: it is essential that the expertise of the biomedics and the physicians in general be seen to qualify them as constituting, as a corps, a respected and trusted and trustworthy co-sovereign in the sacred condominium with the patients or their specialized advocates.

And over the doorway into the condominial chamber of laboratory or hospital I see inscribed rather than the great juramental words of the Pythagorian medical lodge out of which our medical tradition was fashioned, beginning with Hippocrates of Cos, the monitory words of Shakespeare's Cressida of Troy on the Asia Minor mainland a few miles from Cos: "Blind fear, that seeing reason leads, finds safer footing than blind reason stumbling without fear. To fear the worst oft cures the worse."[30]

Notes

Chapter One

1. J. Noonan, *Contraception: A History of Its Treatment by the Catholic Theologians and Canonists,* 92-95 (1965).
2. *Id.* at 10-18.
3. *Id.* at 59, 73-74.
4. *Id.* at 85-91.
5. *Id.* at 56-67.
6. *Id.* at 74-77.
7. *Id.* at 107-10.
8. *Id.* at 119-30.
9. *Id.* at 84, 128, 278-79.
10. *Id.* at 408-9, 490.
11. *Gaudium et spes,* reprinted in Concilii Oecumenici Vaticani II Constitutiones, Decreta Declarations, Sec. 49 (Romita ed., 1967). Paul VI, *Humanae Vitae,* reprinted in 60 Acta Apostolicae Sedis, Sec. 14 (1968).
12. *Humanae Vitae,* reprinted in 60 Acta Apostolica Sedis, Sec. 12 (1968).
13. *Id.* at Sec. 16.
14. *Id.* at Sec. 16.
15. Noonan, *Natural Law, The Teaching of the Church and the Regulation of Human Fecundity,* 25 American Journal of Jurisprudence, 29-37 (1980).
16. Noonan, *An Almost Absolute Value in History,* The Morality of Abortion, 8-9 (1970).
17. *Id.* at 9-10.
18. *Id.* at 26-31 (moralists) and 223 (law).
19. *Id.* at 224-25.
20. *Id.* at 40-42.
21. Noonan, *A Private Choice, Abortion in America in the Seventies,* 5-9, 33-46 (1979).
22. K. Barth, 3 *Church Dogmatics,* 415-22 (1961).
23. A. Gide, *Last Journals,* reprinted in Translation, Winter 1979, at 95

161

162   *The Death Decision*

24. See R. Edwards and J. Purdy, *Human Conception in Vitro* (1982).
25. Pius XII, *Allocution to the Second World Congress on Fertility and Sterility,* reprinted in Acta Apostolicae Sedis, 471 (1956).
26. Jones, *A Technique for the Aspiration of Oocytes from Human Ovarian Follicles,* 37 Journal of Fertility and Sterility, 26-29 (1982).
27. Trounson, *Current Perspectives of In Vitro Fertilization and Embryo Transfer,* 1 Clinical Reproduction and Fertility, 56-65 (1982).
28. Jones, *The Program for In Vitro Fertilization at Norfolk,* 38 Journal of Fertility and Sterility, 14-21 (1982).

Chapter Two

1. I am indebted to Rev. Bruce Einspahr of Columbia Bible Church, Pasco, Washington, whose taped message dated November 1981 assisted in exegeting the passages which follow.
2. We need not revive at this point the longstanding debate between creationism and traducianism. Creationism in this context refers not to the creation of the world or of human life, but to the doctrine that whenever a new human life is formed, God creates afresh a new human soul/spirit, whether at the point of conception or at some time thereafter. The traducian view, on the other hand, holds that the soul/spirit is passed down hereditarily from parents to their children in a manner somewhat similar to the passage of physical characteristics. If one accepts the traducian view, the personhood of the unborn child is virtually settled, for the traducian view necessarily requires that the child has a soul/spirit from the point of conception, since he inherited that soul/spirit from his parents. However, the creationist view does not require a different conclusion as to personhood, for one may very well conclude that God creates a new soul/spirit for each person at the point of conception.

I lean strongly to the traducian view. As we have seen, Psalm 51:5 indicates the child has a sin nature from the point of conception, and Ezekiel 18 indicates that the sin nature resides in the soul/spirit. If, as the creationists maintain, God creates a fresh soul for each new child, then according to Psalm 51:5, he must create a sinful soul. This cannot be, for God cannot be the author of sin.

There are several passages used to support creationism. Isaiah 57:16 refers to "the souls which I have made." Zechariah 12:1 declares that "the Lord . . . formeth the spirit of man within him." It may be significant, however, that the Hebrew word for "make" in Isaiah 57:16 is *asah,* meaning to make or accomplish, and the Hebrew word for "formeth" in Zechariah 12:1 is *yatsar,* meaning to form or fit into a mold. If the authors of scripture had meant a new creation of the soul/spirit, they would probably have used the Hebrew word *barah,* which normally means a new or ex nihilo creation. Finally, Ecclesiastes 12:7 reads, "Then shall the dust return to the earth as it was, and the spirit shall return to God who gave it." But the Hebrew word for "gave" is *nahthan*, which is usually translated give but can also mean make, appoint, put, hand up, yield, or deliver. These passages are, therefore, not conclusive evidence that the authors of scripture accepted creationism.

3. For an excellent analysis of this passage, *see* House, *Miscarriage or Premature Birth: Additional Thoughts on Exodus 21:22-25*, 41 Westminster Theological Journal, 105-23 (1978); *See also* C. Keil & F. Delitzsch, *Commentary on the Old Testament* (J. Martin trans., 1975).

4. Compare Ecclesiastes 5:14-15; Jeremiah 20:18; Genesis 25:23-26; and Genesis 38:28-30 with Numbers 12.

5. The above information is generally accepted medical fact. *See*, e.g., G. Bergel and C. Koop, *When You Were Formed in Secret*, 6 (1980); W. Hamilton and H. Mossman, *Human Embryology*, 188 (1970); T. Humphrey, *The Development of Human Fetal Activity in Its Relation to Postnatal Behavior*, Advances in Child Development and Behavior, 12-19 (W. Reese and L. Lipsitt, eds. 1975); P. Timiras, *Developmental Physiology and Aging* (1972).

6. Paul E. Rockwell, M.D., quoted in G. Burgel and C. Koop, *When You Were Formed in Secret*, 6 (1980).

7. T. Berny and J. Kelly, *The Secret Life of the Unborn Child*, 31 (1981).

8. *Id.* at 23.

9. *Id.* at 23.

10. Diamond, *ISMS Symposium on Medical Implications under the Current Abortion Law in Illinois*, Illinois Medical Journal, 677 (1967).

11. Simms, *A District Attorney Looks at Abortion*, 8, Child and Family, 176-80 (1969).

12. *Abortion and Social Justice*, 48 (D. Horan ed. 1972).

13. Letter from Judge Armand and Della Porta to Sen. Richard Schweiker (July 12, 1977), quoted in *Christian Action Council Resource Manual* SM-18, SM-1M.

14. Groth & Burges, *Sexual Dysfunction During Rape*, The New England Journal of Medicine, 764-66 (1977).

15. *Family Dynamics and Female Sexual Delinquency*, 62 (A. Friman and O. Pollack, eds., 1969).

16. *Christian Action Council Resource Manual*, SM-18, SM-1M.

17. *Id.*

Chapter Three

1. 60 U.S. 393 (1857).

2. 410 U.S. 113 (1973).

3. For a general background discussion on the involvement of American

churches in the slavery controversy, see C. Strout, *The New Heaven and the New Earth: Political Religion in America,* 140-204 (1974).

4. Model Penal Code S230.03 commentary at 428 (official draft 1962).

5. *Constitutional Amendment Guaranteeing Right to Life to the Unborn and Other Persons: Hearings on S.J. Res. 119 and S.J. Res. 130 Before the Subcommittee on Constitutional Amendment of the Senate Committee on the Judiciary,* 93rd Cong., 2d sess. 279 (1974) (Religious Coalition for Abortion Rights, "The Abortion Rights Issue: How We Stand") [hereinafter cited as *Hearings*].

6. *Id.*

7. B. Nathanson and R. Ostling, *Aborting America* (1979) [hereinafter cited as *Nathanson*].

8. *Gaudium et Spes,* reprinted in The Documents of Vatican II, 255-56. (Abbot ed., 1966).

9. *Hearings, supra* note 5, at 227 (Resolution of the National Conference of Catholic Bishops on the Pro-life Constitutional Amendment).

10. *Hearings, supra* note 5, at 231 (Pastoring Guidelines for the Catholic Hospital and Catholic Health Care Personnel).

11. *Id.* at 231-36.

12. *Id.* at 235.

13. *Hearings, supra* note 5, at 158 (Statement of Cardinal John Krol).

14. *Compare Hearings, supra* note 5, at 158 (Statement of Cardinal John Krol indicating a state's rights amendment would not be acceptable).

15. For a discussion of the development of the Catholic position, see D. Granfield, *The Abortion Decision,* 49-74 (1969).

16. *Id.* at 66.

17. *Hearings, supra* note 5, at 136 (Press release from Catholics For a Free Choice, New York, October 20, 1973).

18. *Id.*

19. *Id.*

20. *Hearings, supra* note 5, at 257-58 (Social Principles, General Conference of the United Methodist Church).

21. *Hearings, supra* note 5, at 256 (Testimony of James A. Armstrong, Bishop, the Dakota Area, North Central Jurisdiction, and President, the Board of Church and Society).

22. *Id.*

23. D. Granfield, *supra* note 15, at 67.

24. *Hearings, supra* note 5, at 343 (Letter to Rev. Robert Holbrook from Dr. Albert C. Outler, March 1, 1974).

25. *Hearings, supra* note 5, at 350 (Statement of Paul Ramsey).

26. *Id.* at 351.

27. *Id.* at 355.

28. T.J. Bosgras, *Abortion, the Bible and the Church,* 32-35 (1980).

29. *Hearings, supra* note 5, at 257 (1970 statement of the Lutheran Church in America).
30. *Hearings, supra* note 5, at 571 (Statement of George H. Muedking, Editor of the Lutheran Standard).
31. *Id.*
32. *Id.*
33. Almen and McLellan, *With a New Song: Go and Tell the Story,* Lutheran Standard, Oct. 28, 1980, at 15, col. 2.
34. *Id.* at 15, col. 2-3.
35. *Id.* at 15, col. 3.
36. *Id.*
37. *Id.*
38. *Id.* at 15, col. 3.
39. *Id.* at 16, col. 1.
40. *Id.*
41. *Id.*
42. *Hearings, supra* note 5, at 571 (Statement of George H. Muedking, Editor of the Lutheran Standard).
43. *Hearings, supra* note 5, at 320 (Testimony of Jean Garton, Member of the Board for Social Concern, Lutheran Church-Mo. Synod).
44. *Hearings, supra* note 5, at 321 (Abortion—Theological, Legal, and Medical Aspects, A Report of the Commission on Theological and Church Relations, Lutheran Church-Mo. Synod).
45. *Id.*
46. *Id.* at 323.
47. *Id.* at 322.
48. *Id.* at 323.
49. *Id.* at 326.
50. *Hearings, supra* note 5, at 339 (Statement of Rev. Robert Holbrook, Coordinator of Baptists for Life).
51. *Id.*
52. *Hearings, supra* note 5, at 266 (A Social Pronouncement of the Presbyterian Church in the U.S. adopted by the 1970 General Assembly).
53. *Hearings, supra* note 5, at 360 (Statement adopted by the 182nd General Assembly of the United Presbyterian Church in 1970).
54. *Hearings, supra* note 5, at 362 (Resolution adopted at the 1970 National Meeting of the United Presbyterian Women).
55. *Hearings, supra* note 5, at 264 (Testimony of Jane Stitt, laywoman, teacher at Abilene Christian College, a member of the task force to study abortion established by the Presbyterian Church in the U.S.).
56. *Hearings, supra* note 5, at 268 (A Social Pronouncement of the Presbyterian Church in the U.S. adopted by the 1970 General Assembly).
57. *Hearings, supra* note 5, at 361 (Statement adopted by the 184th General

Assembly of the United Presbyterian Church in 1972).

58. *Hearings, supra* note 5, at 361 (Report on Sexuality and the Human Community, recommended for study and appropriate action by the 182nd General Assembly of the United Presbyterian Church in 1970).

59. *Id.*

60. *Id.* at 362.

61. *Hearings, supra* note 5, at 378 (*Let's Look at Abortion*).

62. *Hearings, supra* note 5, at 378 (Statement of Dr. Robert V. Moss and Dr. Howard E. Spragg of the United Church of Christ).

63. *Id.*

64. *Id.* at 374.

65. *Hearings, supra* note 5, at 617 (Statement of Rev. Albert W. Kovacs of the United Church of Christ).

66. *Hearings, supra* note 5, at 269 (Statement of Rabbi Balfour Brickner, Director of the New York Federation of Reformed Synagogues, Union of American Hebrew Congregations).

67. *Hearings, supra* note 5, at 270 (Mishnah Ohalot 7.6).

68. *Hearings, supra* note 5, at 279 (Religious Coalition for Abortion Rights— *The Abortion Rights Issue, How We Stand*).

69. *Hearings, supra* note 5, at 287 (Statement of Rabbi J. David Bleich, Rabbinical Council of America).

70. *Id.* at 289.

71. *Id.* at 316.

72. *Id.* at 296.

73. *Id.* at 304-5.

74. *Id.* at 295.

75. *Id.* at 310-11.

76. *Id.* at 310-11.

77. *Id.* at 310.

78. *Id.* at 317.

79. *Id.*

80. *Hearings, supra* note 5, at 329-30 (Testimony of Rev. Holbrook).

81. *Id.* at 329.

82. Nathanson, *supra* note 7, at 298.

83. T.J. Bosgras, *supra* note 28, at 39.

84. *Id.* at 41.

85. *Hearings, supra* note 5 at 340 (Statement of Rev. Robert Holbrook).

86. *Hearings, supra* note 5, at 712 (Statement of Rev. Edward O. DeBary).

87. *Id.*

88. B. Nathanson, *supra* note 7, at 300.

89. *Id.*

90. T.J. Bosgras, *supra* note 10, at 70.

91. B. Nathanson, *supra* note 7, at 300.

92. *Hearings, supra* note 5, at 713-14 (Statement of Rev. Edward O. DeBary).
93. *Id.*

Chapter Four

1. *Griswold v. Connecticut,* 381 U.S. 479, 484 (1965).
2. *Roe v. Wade,* 410 U.S. 113, 165 (1973).
3. *Doe v. Bolton,* 410 U.S. 179, 191-192 (1973).
4. Byrn, *An American Tragedy: The Supreme Court on Abortion,* 41 Fordham Law Review, 807, 857-58 (1973).
5. Reilly, *A Wrongful Life,* Medical Times, Sept. 1982 at 119.
6. *See, Jacobs v. Theimer,* 519 S.W. 2nd 846 (Tex. 1975); *Dumer v. St. Michael's Hospital,* 69 Wis. 2d 766, 233 N.W. 2d 372 (1975).
7. 57 App. Div. 2d 73, 394 N.Y.S. 2d 933 (1977).
8. 46 N.Y. 2d 401 (1978).
9. *See, e.g., Sherlock v. Stillwater Clinic,* 260 N.W. 2d 169 (Minn. 1977).
10. Greenfield, *Wrongful Birth: What Is The Damage?,* 248 Journal of the American Medical Association, 926, 927 (1982).
11. 227 A. 2d 689 (N.J. Sup. Ct. 1967).
12. 106 Cal. App. 3rd 811, 165 Cal. Rptr. 477 (1980).
13. *Id.* at 489.
14. *Id.* at 488.
15. Boston Globe, Oct. 15, 1981.
16. Stats. 1981, ch. 331. 51; California Civil Code, Sect. 43.6.
17. *Turpin v. Sortini,* 643 P. 2d 954 (Cal. 1982).
18. *Id.* at 961.
19. 98 Wn. 2d 460, 656 P. 2d 483 (1983).
20. *Id.* at 491.
21. *Id.* at 496.
22. *Robak v. U.S.,* 658 F. 2d 471, 475-476 (7th Cir. 1981).
23. Chicago Tribune, April 21, 1982.
24. Washington Post, May 7, 1982.
25. 410 U.S. at 157, for 54.

Chapter Five

1. *See* Robertson, *Involuntary Euthanasia of Defective Newborns: A Legal Analysis,* 27 Stanford Law Review, 213, 214 (1975).
2. Duff and Campbell, *Moral and Ethical Dilemmas in the Special-Care Nursery,* 289 New England Journal of Medicine, 890 (1973).
3. *When Doctors Play God. (Medicine's gains nullify its ethical quandaries: Who lives, who dies—and who decides?)* Newsweek, Aug. 31, 1981.
4. This detection and prevention of genetic diseases is becoming ever more

advanced. Genetic diseases such as rhesus disease, spina bifida, German measles, sickle-cell anemia, can all be detected three months into pregnancy and treated prenatally so that their effects on the child are negligible. This poses problems for the abortion mentality since in solving such problems by eliminating the victims, it refuses to recognize the fetus as a patient or as a person. *See, Genetic Diseases Can Now Be Detected, Treated Before Birth,* Houston Chronicle, Nov. 26, 1982, at sec. 4, p. 44.

5. There have appeared many studies in this area of death and its evaluation. *See* Philippe Ariès, *The Hour of Our Death* (1981).

6. For perceptive views in this regard, *see* I. Illich, *Medical Nemesis* (1978).

7. St. John-Stevas, *Life, Death and Law*, 264 (1961).

8. This view of life in the Western world started with the Renaissance and continues today in the various secular humanisms (secularism, Fascism, Marxism, etc.). Each of these describes the universe differently, but each is a self-enclosed system with no reference beyond itself. The basis on which all humanisms of the nineteenth and twentieth centuries rest ultimate value is the free, self-developing, possessive individual, insofar as freedom is seen as a possession, namely, a freedom from any but economic relations with others. The ultimate rootlessness of the genderless and possessive individual must be found here where so much of modern despair finds its modern origins. *See* C. MacPherson, *The Political Theory of Possessive Individualism: Hobbes to Locke* (1966).

9. *See Termination of Medical Treatment,* 3 Journal of Legal Medicine, 211 (1982).

10. Illich, *supra* note 6 at 25-30.

11. *See,* A. Solzhenitsyn, *A World Split Apart,* National Review, July 8, 1978, at 115-18.

12. In many respects, the contemporary medical establishment is inevitably a major threat to health. Cf. Bradshaw, *Doctors On Trial* (1979). Each culture, for instance, has its own characteristic way of enjoying pleasure and suffering discomfort, pain, or the fear of death. *See* Buytendijk, *Pain, Its Modes and Functions* (1962).

13. Having taken away their power and ability to deal with their health by professional doctors, these elderly are now led down the illusionary path of health by professional modern counselors of exercise fads and health ("natural") food fetishes. Behind these fundamental denials is modern humanism's inability to integrate the concepts of pain, suffering, growing old, and death within its system. This is what every culture must do if it is to give the individual any meaning whatever. The manifestation of all these fads and fashions are all, therefore, evidence of modern and secular despair or its inability to deal with the totality of life.

14. C. Lasch, *Narcissism,* 11-24 (1978).

15. Ariés, *supra* note 5 at 281-85.
16. For an incisive view of family in its turning point of the modern period (confusion of childhood, gender, sex, etc.), *see* P. Aries, *Centuries of Childhood* (1979). For a discussion of the process by which the proto-industrial mill and the police converge to break down the gendered couple and replace it with the model of the sexual polarization of functions, *see* J. Donzelot, *The Policing of Families* (1979).
17. For a more complete summary, *see* Commercial News (Dansville, Ill.), Oct. 25, 1981, at 3.
18. *Id.*
19. Riga, *Phillip Becker: Another Milestone*, America, July 12, 1980, at 8-9.
20. For a detailed account, *see* Meyers, *Medico-Legal Implications of Death and Dying*, 44-45 (Cumulative Supplement, 1972). The basis of this "opinion" (there really was only a judgment upholding the parents' decision) was not Down's syndrome. This is highly suspicious. Medical and hospital personnel as well as the courts themselves refused to elaborate in any significant way. Since the case was highly publicized and the public outcry very great, there was a duty to the public on the part of these authorities to explain these "insurmountable medical problems." In fact, what little we know points to the opposite conclusion.
21. *Moral and Ethical Dilemmas in the Special Care Nursery*, 289 New England Journal of Medicine 890 (1973). *See also*, Campbell & Duff, *Deciding the Care of Severely Malformed or Dying Infants*, 5 Journal of Medical Ethics, 65 (1979); Fost, *Counseling Families Who Have a Child with a Severe Congenital Anomaly*, 67 Pediatrics, 321 (1981); Jonsen, *Critical Issues in Newborn Intensive Care: A Conference Report and Policy Proposal*, 55 Pediatrics, 756 (1975); Robertson, *Discretionary Non-Treatment of Defective Newborns*, in *Genetics and the Law*, 451 (A. Milunsky & G. Annas, eds., 1976); Shatten & Chabon, *Decision Making and the Right to Refuse Lifesaving Treatment for Defective Newborns*, 3 Journal of Legal Medicine, 59 (1982).
22. No. 74-145 (Superior Ct., Cumberland Cty, Me.), February 14, 1974.
23. This ability of the law is severely restricted, and, in general, it should be. The law is a blunt instrument in trying to decide the delicate medical-moral problems involved in these cases. Only in the most blatant cases, e.g., where a child is allowed to die simply because he or she is retarded, should courts intervene and investigate.
24. Various criteria have been used to determine when "extraordinary" measures are to be discontinued. One suggested by Richard McCormick is that quality of life means to be able to live a life of loving and being loved. If one's potential for that is ended or is so burdened with the mere struggle for survival, then, he argues, it has reached its fullness and all procedures—outside of those to give basics to make the patient

comfortable—should be discontinued. McCormick, *To Save or Let Die,* 229 Journal of the American Medical Association, 172 (1974).

25. Courts have asked for legislative standards but have been forced to set up their own. *See e.g. Lovato v. District Ct.,* 198 Colo. 419, 601 P.2d 1072 (1979); *Satz v. Perlmutter,* 326 So.2d 160 (Fla. App. 1978), *approved,* 379 So.2d 359 (Fla. 1980); *In re Storar,* 52 N.Y.2d 363, 438 N.Y.S.2d 266 (1981).

26. Riga, *supra* note 19, *supra* note 21 at 9.

27. Cf. Zuk, *The Religious Factor and the Role of Guilt in Acceptance of the Retarded Child,* 64 American Journal of Mental Deficiency, 139 (1959).

28. P. Foot, *Euthanasia,* 6 Philosophy and Public Affairs, 87 (1977).

29. *In re Quinlan,* 70 N.J. 10, 355 A.2d 647 (1976). *See also The Ad hoc Committee of the Harvard Medical School to Examine the Definition of Brain Death, A Definition of Irreversible Coma,* reprinted in 205 Journal of the American Medical Association, 205 (1968). These criteria have since been expanded. *See* Relman, *The Saikewicz Decision: A Medical Viewpoint,* 4 American Journal of Law and Medicine, 233 (1978); Schram, *No Code: Clarification in the Aftermath of Saikewicz,* 299 New England Journal of Medicine, 875 (1978).

30. *See* Gustofson, *Mongolism, Parental Desires, and the Right to Life,* 16 Perspectives in Biology and Medicine, 524, 529-33 (1973); Silverman, *Mismatched Attitudes about Neonatal Death,* 11 The Hastings Center Report, 12 (1981).

31. *See Termination of Medical Treatment, supra* note 9 at 233-38.

32. Darling, *Parents, Physicians and Spina Bifida,* 7 The Hastings Center Report, 11, 13 (1977).

33. *See supra* note 28.

34. *Id.* at 145.

35. Lazar and Orpet, *Attitudes of Young Gifted Boys and Girls toward Handicapped Individuals,* 38 Exceptional Children, 489-90 (1972).

36. Fletcher, *Attitudes toward Defective Newborns,* 2 Hastings Center Studies, 21, 27 (1974).

37. Reid, *Spina Bifida: The Fate of the Untreated,* 7 The Hastings Center Report, 16, 19 (1977).

38. Robertson, *supra* note 1, at 266.

39. The following criteria are gleaned in part from the articles already cited in these notes. While not definitive in nature, they may continue a dialog already begun in the medico-legal literature.

Chapter Seven

1. W. Friedmann, *Legal Theory,* 253-311 (5th ed., 1967). Generally speaking, one's view on the nature of law significantly affects one's

interpretation of legal materials and human dynamics. The subject area of this essay presents a prime example of an area in which formal and informal dynamics are closely interwoven.

2. Historically, Eugene Erhlich was the leading figure to explore the various levels and kinds of law, W. Friedmann, *supra* note 1 at 246-52. There is a real sense in which some of the norms of medicine are a kind of law. Such norms help to determine, for instance, whether a physician is liable for causing damage to a patient. To the extent courts defer such norms, say regarding the withholding of resuscitative measures from a terminal patient, the medical norms are the "law in action."

3. This essay deals only tangentially with the questions relating to seriously ill newborns. See further, Robertson, *Involuntary Euthanasia of Defective Newborn: A Legal Analysis,* 27 Stanford Law Review, 213 (1975); T.S. Ellis, *Letting Defective Babies Die: Who Decides?* 7 American Journal of Law and Medicine, 393 (1982). Of course, the questions of that area and those of this essay are related, as are questions concerning abortion.

4. Clarke, *The Choice to Refuse or Withhold Medical Treatment: The Emerging Technology and Medical-Ethical Consensus,* 13 Creighton Law Review 795 (1980); note, *The Refusal of Life-Saving Medical Treatment vs. the State's Interest in Preservation of Life: A Clarification of the Interests at Stake,* 58 Washington University Law Quarterly, 85 (1980).

5. A thorough discussion of the mix of law and ethics involved in informed consent is available in "Making Health Care Decisions: The Ethical and Legal Implications of Informed Consent in the Patient-Practitioner Relationship," a report from the President's Commission for the Study of Ethical Problems in Medicine and Biomedical Behaviorial Research, issued October 1982. The general sense of the report is that law should play a supporting or reenforcement role to promote "shared decision-making," *e.g.,* p. 30. According to the Report, informed consent "is essentially an ethical imperative," p. 2.

6. The most notable distinction is between "actively" causing death and "passively" letting it happen. This distinction has some merit as one conclusory of moral values, but not where one person has a duty not to let another person die. See discussion in "Deciding to Forego Life-Sustaining Treatment," partial revised draft of the President's Commission for the Study of Ethical Problems in Medicine and Biomedical and Behavioral Research, November 1982, at ch. 2, pp. 28-50. Perhaps a more slippery distinction is between "ordinary" and "extraordinary" means of medical intervention. The Presidential Commission is heavily critical of this distinction, ch. 2, pp. 55-62, labelling it as mainly conclusory of value and policy judgments often not articulated. There are other definitional problems, *e.g.,* "terminal," "right to die," "euthanasia," "substituted judgment," and so forth.

7. Veatch, *Death and Dying: The Legislative Options,* The Hastings Center Report, 5 (October 1977); Lappe, *Dying While Living: A Critique of Allowing to Die Legislation,* 4 Journal of Medical Ethics, 195 (1978); Dyck, *Living Wills and Mercy Killings: An Ethical Assessment,* in Bioethics and Human Rights (Bandman and Bandman, eds., 1978). The idea of the living will has been judicially legitimated without legislation, *In the Matter of Eichner,* 52 N.Y. 2d 363, 378-80, 420 N.E. 2d 64, 72 (Ct. of Ap. 1981).

8. Baron, *Assuring "Detached But Passionate Investigation and Decision": The Role of Guardians Ad Litem in Saikewicz-Type Cases,* 4 American Journal of Law and Medicine, 337 (1979). In Massachusetts, such review is required in the case of incompetents who are wards of the state or without caring relatives: *Superintendent of Belchertown State School v. Saikewicz,* 370 N.E. 2d 417 (1977); Custody of a Minor, 434 N.E. 2d 601 (Mass. 1982). The view against judicial review is stated in Relman, *The Saikewicz Decision: A Response to Allen Buchanan's Views on Decision-Making for Terminally Ill Incompetents,* 5 American Journal of Law and Medicine, 119 (1979).

9. Whether a patient is dying or not is a medical question. Whether a person can be kept from dying is also. Whether such a person should be kept from dying is not. There are situations in which these lines may be clear. Courts have no business in reviewing the case of a person who is dying and cannot be saved. Even where the lines are tangled, sometimes the only persons realistically who can call the shots are the attending physicians, where feasible in collaboration with the patient or relatives. See *"Does 'Doing Everything' include CPR?" Case Study,* 12 The Hastings Center Report, No. 5, p. 27 (October 1982); Miles, Cranford, and Schultz, *The Do-Not Resuscitate Order in a Teaching Hospital,* 96 Annals of Internal Medicine, 660, 664 (1982); *Letters on Code or No-Code,* 300 New England Journal of Medicine, 1057 (1979).

10. *Eichner v. Dillon,* 73 A.D. 431, 426 N.Y. S2d 517, 543 (1980).

11. *In Re Quinlan,* 70 N.J. 10, 355 A.2d 647, *cert. den.,* 429 U.S. 922 (1976); *Superintendent of Belchertown State School v. Saikewicz,* 373 Mass. 728, 370 N.E. 2d 417 (1977); *Satz v. Perlmutter,* 379 So.2d 359 (Fla. 1980). Delgado, *Euthanasia Reconsidered: The Choice of Death as an Aspect of the Right of Privacy,* 17 Arizona Law Review, 474 (1975). Against such an analysis, note, *The Tragic Choice: Termination of Care for Patients in a Permanent Vegetative State,* 51 New York University Law Review, 285 (1976).

12. *In the Matter of Earle Spring,* 405 N.E. 2d 115 (Mass., 1980), discussed in Annas, *Quality of Life in the Courts: Earle Spring in Fantasyland,* The Hastings Center Report, Aug., 1980, p. 9.

13. *Superintendent of Belchertown State School v. Saikewicz,* 373 Mass. 728,

370 N.E. 2d 417 (1977).

14. *In the Matter of Dinnerstein,* 380 N.E. 2d 134 (1978). Some of the medical community's reaction to *Saikewicz* is described in Curran and Shapiro, *Law, Medicine and Forensic Science,* 838–39 (Little, Brown & Co., 3rd ed., 1982).

15. Thus *Saikewicz* was interpreted in a limited fashion and confirmed in the case of an abandoned infant which was a ward of the state, *Custody of a Minor,* 434 N.E. 2d 601 (Mass. 1982).

16. See Ellis, *Letting Defective Babies Die: Who Decides?,* 7 American Journal of Law and Medicine, 393 (1982), making much of the lack of such standards.

17. Prosser, *Law of Torts,* 103 (4th ed., 1971).

18. The leading quote is from Justice Cardozo: "Every human being of adult years and sound mind has a right to determine what shall be done with his own body." *Schloendorff v. Society of New York Hospitals,* 211 N.Y. 125, 129, 105 N.E. 2d 92, 93 (1914).

19. *See supra* note 5. The leading malpractice case is *Cobb v. Grant,* 8 Cal. 3d 229, 502 P.2d 1, 104 Cal. Rptr. 505 (1972). See generally, Clarke, *The Choice to Refuse or Withhold Medical Treatment,* 13 Creighton Law Review, 795, 797 (1980).

20. Wesley Hohfeld provided the seminal analysis calling attention to the confusing and misleading ambiguity of the term "right" as used in law, *e.g., Some Fundamental Legal Conceptions as Applied to Judicial Reasoning* (1913).

21. *See supra* note 11.

22. 410 U.S. 113 (1973).

23. *See* Professor Noonan's assertion that *Roe v. Wade* has by subsequent interpretation come to stand for the pregnant woman's having a right to an abortion, chapter 1, above. Cf. The Supreme Court's reaffirmation that what is involved is the woman's right of privacy which "is broad enough to encompass a woman's decision whether or not to terminate her pregnancy," *Roe v. Wade,* 410 U.S. 113, 153, quoted in *Planned Parenthood of Central Missouri v. Danforth,* 428 U.S. 52 (1976).

24. Of course our law has never treated the value of life as an absolute, as witness the justifications involved in support of capital punishment and the privilege of self-defense.

25. The courts have not stated the right as absolute, always suggesting it involves a balance of interests, *Satz v. Perlmutter,* 362 So.2d 160 (Fla. App. 1978), particularly if refusal of treatment would involve abandonment of a dependent child, *Application of the President and Directors of Georgetown College, Inc.,* 118 U.S. App. D.C. 80, 331 F. 2d 1000, *cert. denied,* 377 U.S. 978 (1964). In *Commissioner of Corrections v. Myers,* 399 N.E. 2d 452 (Mass. 1979), a prisoner in his twenties was denied the right

to refuse dialysis as against the interest of the state in controlling the administration of the prison system.

The true test would be the case in which a person might be perceived as using his temporarily critical condition as a means of ending his life despite a quality of life expectation that observers would see as not morally justifying the decision.

26. *In re Quinlan,* 70 N.J. 10, 355A.2d 647 (1976).

27. Its strength lay in the evidence of the father's close and caring relationship with Karen and with his apparent moral character.

28. Opinions of the American Judicial Council of the American Medical Association, No. 211 (1982) state: "Where a terminally ill patient's coma is beyond doubt irreversible. . . . all means of life support may be discontinued." The New York Court of Appeals has stopped short of this position *In the Matter of Eichner,* 52 N.Y. 2d 363, 420 N.E. 2d 64, 438 NYS 2d 266 (1981), but the case involved clear evidence that the patient wanted life support removed in the event of his suffering irreversible coma.

29. In a somewhat similar situation to that of *Saikewicz,* the New York Court of Appeals rejected the substituted judgment approach as "unrealistic," *In the Matter of Storar,* 52 N.Y. 2d 362, 420 N.E. 2d 64, 438 NYS 2d 266 (1981). Subsequently the Massachusetts high court noted the *Storar* rejection but reaffirmed its own allegiance to the substituted judgment approach as preferable to the alternative "best interest" of the patient approach, *In the Matter of Roe,* 432 N.E. 2d 712 (1982). See a criticism of the substituted judgment analysis in Ramsey, *The Saikewicz Precedent: What Good for an Incompetent Patient,* 8 The Hastings Center Report, No. 6, p. 36 (Dec. 1978).

30. The approach taken in *Storar, supra* note 29, with a severely mentally retarded "adult."

31. The *Opinions of the American Judicial Council of the American Medical Association,* No. 210 (1982), would take the best interest of the patient approach: "Quality of life is a factor to be considered in determining what is best for the individual. Life should be cherished despite disabilities and handicaps, except when prolongation would be inhumane and unconscionable. Under these circumstances, withholding or removing life supporting means is ethical provided that normal care given an individual who is ill is not discontinued."

See the discussion of both the "substituted judgment" and "best interest" approaches in the partial revised draft of "Deciding to Forego Life-Sustaining Treatment," ch. 4, pp. 28-40, of the President's Commission for the Study of Ethical Problems in Medicine and Biomedical and Behavioral Research, November 1982.

32. See discussion of the Ethics Committee approach in the Report of the

President's Commission, *supra* note 31, Ch. IV, pp. 28-40.

33. *See* Prof. Williams's paper and discussion of an "Ethics Condominium," chapter 8 below. The President's Commission would mandate some such body if life support is to be withheld from a newborn, *supra* note 31, at ch. 6, pp. 31-32.

Chapter Eight

1. Jonathan Leonard, "The First Genetic Engineers: Human tinkering with bacteria now seems far less menacing than what the bacteria are doing on their own," *Harvard Magazine,* November-December 1982, pp. 36-41.

2. Lucian, *The Disinherited,* p. 23; quoted by Darrel W. Amundsen. See below, note 3.

3. Darrel W. Amundsen, "Casuistry and Professional Obligations: The Regulation of Physicians by the Court of Conscience in the Late Middle Ages," *Transactions and Studies of the College of Physicians and Surgeons of Philadelphia,* 3, No. 2 (March 1981), pp. 22-39; ibid., No. 3 (June 1981), pp. 93-112.

4. Quoted by Amundsen, "Casuistry," p. 31. Also note 46.

5. An observation of Walter Probert, in "Legal and Ethical Dilemmas," chapter 7 above, not said in necessary approbation of the trend.

6. For morality plays and masques on the stage, fear was sometimes personified as a frightening shrouded figure, in Cressida's words led onto the stage of life by illumed or seeing reason: "Blind fear, that seeing reason leads, finds safer footing than blind reason stumbling without fear."

7. The lengthy document with ten propositions is contained in *Trials of War Criminals,* No. 10, vol. 2 (Washington, D.C., 1949). It is accessible in its essence in Stanley Saul Reiser, Arthur S. Dyck, and William J. Curran, eds., *Ethics in Medicine: Historical Perspectives and Contemporary Concerns* (Cambridge and London: M.I.T. Press, 1977). It is summarized further and placed in context by George H. Kieffer, *Bioethics: A Textbook of Issues* (Reading, Mass.: Addison-Wesley, 1979), esp. p. 239. For the Nazi context, see A. Metscherlick and F. Mulke, *Doctors and Infamy* (New York: Schumann, 1949), which also contains the ten points of the Nuremberg Code.

8. *Psychiatry,* vol. 45, Nov. 1982, pp. 283-97. On the aura and mystique of the hospital protocol as self-protection, see Lifton's forthcoming book of the same title.

9. Though the provision against abortion in the Hippocratic oath and the Declaration of Geneva remained in force in the Federal Republic of Germany and as part of its Constitution, the Declaration of Oslo of 1970 made this provision contingent.

10. The findings are edited by the convener, Hans-Ruedi Weber, *Experiments with Man,* WCCC Studies, No. 6 (Geneva and New York, 1969). The

German edition is *Experimente Menschen.*

11. In a letter to the present author of 1 October 1982, Professor Potter wrote: "Yes, I believe that there can be no doubt that I was the first to use the term bioethics, since the manuscript for the book was in the hands of the publisher, using the term in the title, early in 1970."

12. Cf. K. Danner Clouser, "Bioethics," in *Encyclopedia of Bioethics,* 4 vols., ed. Warren T. Reich, New York: Free Press; London: Macmillan, 1978).

13. See, for example, Paul Ramsey, *The Patient as Person* (New Haven: Yale University Press, 1970); Robert Grungs, S.J., "Human Life vs. Human Personhood," *The Human Life Review* 8, No. 3 (Summer 1982), pp. 70-85.

14. I have dealt with this in Vatican II and in the present pontificate in *The Mind of John Paul II: Origins of His Thought and Action* (New York: Seabury Press, 1981), chapter 10, parts 1 and 5.

15. Although here in the specific sphere of homosexuality, this and the whole chapter with the passage from Mars Hill and other passages in the New Testament sufficiently justify as Christian a resort to the elucidation of natural law and the observance of its restraints in any context.

16. I first felt the awe of this generalization at an address by Prof. Carroll Williams, M.D., of Harvard at Adams House, 27 October 1982; see comprehensively Ernst Mayer, *The Growth of Biological Thought: Diversity, Evolution, and Inheritance* (Cambridge: Belknap Press, 1982).

17. Darrel Amundsen, "The Physician's Obligation to Prolong Life: A Medical Duty without Classical Roots," *Report of the Hastings Institute of Social Ethics and the Life Sciences* (Hastings on Hudson, N.Y., August 1978), p. 24; D. Amundsen and Gary B. Ferngren, "Philanthropy in Medicine: Some Historical Perspectives," in *Beneficience and Health Care,* ed. Earl E. Shelp (Dordrecht: D. Reidel, 1982).

18. *De augmentis scientiarum libri ix* (1623), Book 4; noted in Amundsen, "Obligation."

19. Ludwig Edelstein, *The Hippocratic Oath* (Baltimore: Johns Hopkins University Press, 1943). Not in agreement but with less satisfactory explanations is Fridolf Kulien, "Medical Ethics and Popular Ethics in Greece and Rome," *Clio Medica* 5 (1970), pp. 91-121.

20. Albert R. Jonsen, "Do No Harm: Axiom of Medical Ethics," *Philosophical and Medical Ethics: Its Nature and Significance, Proceedings of the Third Trans-Disciplinary Symposium on Philosophy and Medicine, Farmington, Connecticut, 11-13 December 1975,* ed. Stuart F. Spicker and H. Tristam Engelhardt, reprinted in *Philosophy and Medicine,* same editors, vol. 3 (Dordrecht and Boston: Reidel, 1977), pp. 27-41. This axiom is not part of the Hippocratic oath but part of the Hippocratic Corpus, I, cap. 11, of the *Epidemics,* which almost certainly comes from Hippocrates on his rounds (*epidemia*). The Oath of Hippocrates and other works of his or ascribed to him are available in the *Opera* in Greek and English, tr. by

W.H.S. Jones, 4 vols., Loeb Classical Library (Cambridge and London: Harvard University Press, 1923), vol 1, pp. 291-301. Important selections from the works, including the Oath, are accessible in *Ethics in Medicine,* ed. Stanley Joel Reiser et al. (Cambridge and London: M.I.T. Press, 1977), pp. 5-9.

21. Hippocrates, *Opera,* II, p. 193.
22. In the Declaration of Geneva, 1948, it reads: ". . . the health of my patient will be my first consideration."
23. Joseph Fletcher, *Humanhood: Essays in Biomedical Ethics* (Buffalo: Prometheus Books, 1979). The collected essays cover publications from 1968 to 1978 and embrace all the major problems of microbioethics as well as suicide and topics relating to macrobioethics. With the same intent as Fletcher, but under the axiom "the patient's interest," Jan Hendrick van den Berg, in *Medical Power and Medical Ethics* (Dutch ed., 1969; English trans., York and Toronto: Norton, 1978), distinguishing between closed body/open body medicine, argues against grossly mutilating operations.
24. See the strictures made by Hans Jonas, "Philosophical Reflections on Experimenting with Human Subjects" (1970) and "Against the Stream: Comments on the Definition and Redefinition of Death" (1970, updated), in *Philosophical Essays, From Ancient Creed to Technological Man* (Chicago/London: University of Chicago Press, 1974), chapters 5 and 6.
25. Printed in *The Journal of the American Medical Association* 205 (1968), pp. 337-40, reprinted in Reiser et al., *Bioethics,* pp. 504-7. The present author had to decline the invitation of the chairman, Henry K. Beecher, M.D., as a representative of the Harvard Divinity School.
26. *Osservatore Romano,* 24 October 1982, p. 2.
27. I first introduced this concept in "Religious Residues and Presuppositions in the American Debate on Abortion," *Theological Studies* 31 (Woodstock, Md., 1970), pp. 10-75; part two of which was reprinted as "The Sacred Condominium," *The Morality of Abortion: Legal and Historical Perspectives,* ed. John Noonan, Jr. (Cambridge: Harvard University Press, 1970), pp. 146-71; third printing in paperback, 1972. The long article, partly historical, partly theoretical and ethical, was worked out before the Supreme Court decision on *Roe v. Wade* of 22 January 1973, when the author was almost certain that the Court would find the fetus a person as, by amendments to the Constitution after the Civil War, former slaves were deemed plenary persons in the sense of the Constitution. It was, in part, with a view to returning to the model presented in the article for the larger purposes of bioethics that the author accepted the present assignment at Oral Roberts University.

The condominical model remains intact and extendable even though the original centered in abortion debated before *Roe v. Wade,* when I sought to legitimate certain exceptions in which the mother would have the prevailing voice: incest and rape, within the deliberations of the sacred condominium. I left it with the parents and the physician in the case of a grossly defective fetus detected by amniocentesis. I have since become much more wary of eugenic abortion.

In the historical section of my article, I thought of the resistance to abortion and infanticide as "near constants" in the Judeo-Christian tradition. I said this also in "The Democratization of a Near Constant in History," the foreword to *Abortion and Social Justice*, ed. Thomas W. Hilgers and Dennis J. Horan (New York: Sheed & Ward, 1972), subsidized by the Americans United for Life, of which I was the founding president. More recently in an article by Victor G. Rosenblum and Michael L. Budde, "Historical and Cultural Considerations of Infanticide," in *Infanticide and the Handicapped*, ed. by Denis J. Horan and Melinda Delahoyde (Provo, Utah: Brigham Young University Press, 1982), copyrighted by Americans United for Life, ch. 1, it is evident that infanticide in Christendom until about 1870 was almost as common as in classical antiquity. In the Introduction by Paul Ramsey it is pointed out that infanticide of the handicapped paved the way to the Holocaust of whole races and undesirable classes of the German and vanquished populations, quoting Leo Alexander, "Medical Science under Dictatorship," *New England Journal of Medicine* 39 (1949), p. 241. This suggests that the Nazi nightmare is not just a bad dream, but is capable of replication in American society. However, Ramsey's essay has the logic of a professional ethicist of great repute; and for the whole volume I myself wrote the following commendation: "How a society perceives and treats the senile, the insane, the otherwise handicapped, and life itself still in the womb, also how it deals with the physical and psychological environment in which children are begotten and born and in which their parents labor and might incur for their progeny genetic defects are all major indicators of the degree to which a society approaches plenary humaneness in law, medicine, and public health. Compassion, conscience, and ethical sensibility are put to the test by the details spread before us with the professional concern for the right to life, however severely limited, of children delivered, however severely handicapped. The book is a challenge to all who would prefer to hasten on other good missions on the road down to Jericho."

However, since as many as ten percent of live births are to some degree defective, either by reason of the manner of delivery or because of congenital defects, I still hold that, as abortion is different from infanticide, the parents and the doctor with the consent of the parents have a right which they may exercise, as does nature itself, in intervening at an early stage of fetal misdevelopment that a place in the heart and at the hearth of a family not be preempted by the birth of a detected severely

handicapped embryo that would require lifelong institutional care. What is done in the hospitals of a relatively wealthy society should be deemed applicable to Calcutta, Cairo, and the favelas of Caracas.
28. Ulrich Thomas Lauterbach, *Tractatio de condominio territoriali* (Tübingen, 1682).
29. On this I am normally perhaps slightly more conservative than Bernard Haring, C.SS.R., *Manipulation: Ethical Boundaries of Medical, Behavioral and Genetic Manipulation* (Sough: St. Paul, 1975).
30. That these were cozening words based on a theatrical metaphor does not deprive them of their essential profundity in Shakespeare's most ironic of plays, nor dispossess them of the force they have come to acquire by repeated application apart from the immediate context of the play.